THE LIGHT IN THE DARK TAROT

& ORACLE

Quadrille, Penguin Random House UK,
One Embassy Gardens, 8 Viaduct Gardens,
London SW11 7BW

Quadrille Publishing Limited is part of the
Penguin Random House group of companies
whose addresses can be found at global.
penguinrandomhouse.com

Copyright text © Kerry Ward 2026
Copyright illustrations © Visions in Blue 2026

Kerry Ward has asserted their right to be
identified as the author of this Work in accordance
with the Copyright, Designs and Patents Act 1988

Penguin Random House values and supports
copyright. Copyright fuels creativity, encourages
diverse voices, promotes freedom of expression
and supports a vibrant culture. Thank you for
purchasing an authorised edition of this book
and for respecting intellectual property laws
by not reproducing, scanning or distributing
any part of it by any means without permission.
You are supporting authors and enabling Penguin
Random House to continue to publish books for
everyone. No part of this book may be used or
reproduced in any manner for the purpose of
training artificial intelligence technologies or
systems. In accordance with Article 4(3) of the
DSM Directive 2019/790, Penguin Random House
expressly reserves this work from the text and
data mining exception.

Published by Quadrille in 2026

www.penguin.co.uk

A CIP catalogue record for this book
is available from the British Library

ISBN 978-1-83783-334-4
10 9 8 7 6 5 4 3 2

Publishing Director: Kate Pollard
Editor: Phoebe Bath
Design: Claire Warner Studio
Illustrator: Visions in Blue
Production Controller: Martina Georgieva

Colour reproduction by p2d

Printed in China by RR Donnelley Asia
Printing Solution Limited

The authorised representative in the EEA is
Penguin Random House Ireland, Morrison
Chambers, 32 Nassau Street, Dublin D02 YH68.

Penguin Random House is committed to
a sustainable future for our business, our
readers and our planet. This book is made from
Forest Stewardship Council® certified paper.

Dedicated to my dad
Who taught me to love life

ILLUSTRATIONS BY
VISIONS IN BLUE

KERRY WARD

THE LIGHT IN THE DARK TAROT & ORACLE

TO LEAD YOU TO BRIGHTER TIMES

Quadrille

CONTENTS

To Light Your Way in Dark Times 7
How to Use This Deck 11

THE MAJOR ARCANA — 13

0	The Fool	15
1	The Magician	17
2	The High Priestess	19
3	The Empress	21
4	The Emperor	23
5	The Hierophant	25
6	The Lovers	27
7	The Chariot	29
8	Strength	31
9	The Hermit	33
10	The Wheel of Fortune	35
11	Justice	37
12	The Hanged Man	39
13	Death	41
14	Temperance	43
15	The Devil	45
16	The Tower	47
17	The Star	49
18	The Moon	51
19	The Sun	53
20	Judgement	55
21	The World	57

THE MINOR ARCANA — 59

The Suit of Coins — 60
The Suit of Cups — 74
The Suit of Swords — 88
The Suit of Wands — 102

TAROT SPREADS — 117

Using the Cards as Oracle Cards or Single Card Readings — 119

Using the Cards for Protection — 121

Using the Cards for Encouragement — 123

Using the Cards for Relationship Advice — 125

Using the Cards for a Time-specific Reading — 127

Using the Cards for Home Truths and Personal Development — 129

Numerology — 131
Acknowledgements — 134
About the Author — 135

TO
LIGHT
YOUR WAY
IN DARK
TIMES

> **This tarot deck comes from a very personal place for me. It is the result of a shift in my own life and outlook which, in essence, focuses me on seeking and sharing light, hope, positivity and encouragement.**

I can trace this back to Covid. Those weird, lost years after which nothing has been quite the same – or that's how it feels to me. My dad died in 2020 and, right now, my mum is facing her own illness with great courage. Collectively, we have witnessed the start of wars that show no sign of ending, a climate shift that at times feels apocalyptic, a cost of living (or should that be corporate greed?) crisis that bites into every family and every household. Everyone has their story, I know. We all suffer and struggle.

In the moment, when bad things happen, we endure and we carry on, often because we have little choice. We do the best we can with what is thrown at us and frequently find that things are rarely as intolerable as we fear they might be. Action is far easier to manage than dread. And yet, a toll is taken somehow, over time. A spirit can start to dull.

I started thinking about how to counter this 'creep' of darkness and the Universe showed me some things which provoked me.

At my local natural history museum there is an exhibition for Dr Willard Wigan MBE, who makes incredible miniatures. A poster presides over his mind-bending creations showing a quote from his mum, which reads:

'Encourage people with positivity – you never know where it will take them'. This struck a chord that resonated with me.

A recent trip to Krakow also sparked some thoughts. I love being in churches – the candles, incense, history, the quiet and darkness of the cloisters and chambers, the power of prayer and contemplation. I enjoyed watching people find their comfort, their encouragement, their peace. I felt then and there that I wanted to make a tarot deck that could be used for comfort, like those candles people light when they pray. I wanted to make an offering of comfort and encouragement outside of the ideologies of religion, something to focus on to keep out the shadows. I have always found tarot to be an ally, a guide, a source of truth, comfort and hope.

I wanted to create a deck that served this need and would let no one leave its grasp without feeling encouraged and comforted.

I asked all my clients to talk to me about what encouragement means to them and how they seek it. The responses were fascinating. Some recalled the kindness of strangers and doing good deeds without a thought of any return. Many recommended avoiding social media. Having someone believe in them, especially if that person was strict or demanding, came high on the list. Having a plethora of good books, music and podcasts to be inspired by was deemed important as was, for many, their faith or religion. Then I researched different ways and means of finding positivity and hope, or igniting a change of mood in the moment.

I have distilled all this insight into this deck. Every card carries not just its traditional meaning, but also appropriate words of encouragement, as well as an action you can do right then and there that will make you feel better and embody the energy of that card.

Tarot has been around for over five hundred years, and the cards intrinsically carry the human history, wisdom and experience of those five centuries. You can lean on them; you can rely on them and their knowledge of the human condition. They wish to impart their knowledge to you to encourage you to enjoy the passage of time as best you can and to live with purpose.

I hope this deck will become a source of positivity, hope and light for you; a light in the darkness.

Kerry

I hope this deck will become a source of positivity, hope and light for you: a light in the darkness.

How to Use This Deck

This deck can be used as a straightforward tarot deck and the traditional meanings of the cards are included in this guide, going right through both the Major and Minor Arcana, followed by each card in the four suits: Coins, Cups, Swords and Wands. But that is just the beginning.

Daily oracle message
Each card also carries a daily oracle message. Simply pull one card at a time as and when you need a lift, a boost, a comforting word or some inspiration.

Message of encouragement
This is followed by a message of encouragement appropriate to the chosen card, so that you can focus your mind on an area of your life that may feel lacking, and convince yourself of the strength that you have within you. Quotes from great thinkers demonstrate that the power of following the right course is not constrained by location, ethnicity, gender or any other factors that can otherwise threaten to divide us.

Power words
The power words can be used for focus, meditation or to offer you a starting point to find your unique source of encouragement.

Cosmic force influencing you
Each card in the tarot deck is influenced by cosmic forces relating to a particular area of your life. The Major Arcana link to a planet or zodiac sign, directing you to consider aspects of life, such as work, communication or opportunity. The Minor Arcana link to an element, encouraging you to draw on the strength of that element when you choose a relevant card.

Positive action you can take right now
Every card also carries a ritual or positive action you can perform straightaway, so this tarot deck can also act as a real-life, in-the-moment coach, helping you to take steps to feel better and tackle something useful and proactive.

Tune in to their strength
At the end of the book, you will find instructions on various ways to use the cards, how to conduct the rituals and lay out the cards for reading. There is also full guidance on creating a sacred space for your readings.

The cards are designed specifically to be meditative and ritualistic, almost like prayer cards but without the religious connotations. Choose ones that resonate with you visually, or which carry a message you want to keep close to your heart, and keep those cards on your person, tacked to a mirror, inside your phone or wallet. Make them portable little allies that can accompany you throughout your day and remind you of their motivating and comforting message.

THE MAJOR ARCANA

The Major Arcana are the named and numbered cards in the tarot pack, each of which has specific meanings in a reading. Historically, they are the trump cards, representing the core of a reading.

0 / THE FOOL

The Fool is the first card of the tarot, its ultimate symbol of new beginnings. The Fool enters your realm to bring his energizing enthusiasm to back you to do something new. This new beginning could occur suddenly and be a surprise to those around you, but you knew it was coming. Don't worry about the details or the long term, just make the leap. The Fool will leap with you. Ready?

Daily oracle message
Today is the day that YOU initiate a new life journey or chapter. The biggest step is the decision to act; the rest of the journey is just tenacity and effort.

Message of encouragement
No amount of gold, recognition or favour is as powerful as the ability to change, to turn the page. You hold that power in your hands right now. From here, you can create any life you choose. Feel a deep gratitude that today you are able to make something new, different and better than yesterday.

'Take the first step in faith. You don't have to see the whole staircase, just take the first step.'
Martin Luther King, American religious minister and activist (1929–68)

Power words
Begin, dawn, embark, genesis, new leaf, source, start, take off.

Cosmic force influencing you
The Fool is linked to Uranus, the unpredictable planet of progressive inventions and revolution.

Positive action you can take right now

+ Identify the new beginning you wish to make.

+ Get a clean sheet of paper and a glass of iced water.

+ Light a candle. Fire is transforming and when it is present, we feel emboldened by its flickering light.

+ The paper, the fire's smoke and the water complete the four elements.

+ Write down the first steps you must take to activate this new beginning (no more than three).

+ Drink the water, repeat the steps to yourself, and start as soon as you can.

1/ THE MAGICIAN

The Magician is my personal favourite card. You know the things that made you stand out – weird or wonderful – as a child? They are the secret ingredients of your success as an adult. The magic has been there all long, hardwired in your factory settings, but schooling, making money and day-to-day routines can all dull the shine of your natural glow. Go back to those raw passions, talents and interests of childhood. Reinvent them as adult pursuits. Give yourself permission to discover, invent, create and occupy your own niche in this life. Embrace your uniqueness.

Daily oracle message
Today is the day that YOU step into your talent, your power, your inventiveness, your creativity. The more you do so, the more creativity will flow and the more you will receive. There is a niche in this world just for you. Seek it now.

Message of encouragement
The Magician knows you are unique; there is no other you, there is no other blend of your talent, character, strength and humour. By tapping into your source personality and skill, you can invent something that no one else can do.

*'You can't use up creativity.
The more you use, the more you have.'*
Maya Angelou, American memoirist and poet (1928–2014)

Power words
Conceive, create, design, devise, discover, initiate, innovate, invent.

Cosmic force influencing you
The Magician is linked to Mercury, the creative planet of busy communications, commerce and travel.

Positive action you can take right now
Here are the key creative strengths of the star signs. Does this resonate with you? Look at your sign's strengths and do something today that demonstrates that quality, that flexes that creative muscle, that puts you in that flow.

+ **Fire signs (Leo, Aries, Sagittarius):** Advancing, competing, performing, promoting.

+ **Air signs (Libra, Gemini, Aquarius):** Educating, inventing, researching, writing.

+ **Water signs (Pisces, Scorpio, Cancer):** Inspiring, intuiting, nurturing, performing.

+ **Earth signs (Virgo, Taurus, Capricorn):** Building, constructing, creating, designing.

2/THE HIGH PRIESTESS

The High Priestess is the tarot's divine, feminine power source, and she is sitting with you now, granting you her favour. She wants you to rely on your own gut instinct and intuition. It's likely there's an epiphany coming your way in the next few days, an internal insight that you experience as a 'lightbulb moment'. Be still and quiet and tune in to this power source. Can you spot her elegant presence from the corner of your eye?

Daily oracle message
Today is the day that YOU turn inwards, notice, feel amazed by and learn from your inner flow of insight, inspiration and wisdom. Use today's positive action ritual to do so. Journey into the heart of your being and confront what is there.

Message of encouragement
Deep down, you do know what's right for you. Doubt clouds so much of our thinking. Cast it aside. Clear away the clouds and cobwebs and see the truth without illusion or shadow. From here, your experience and wisdom will guide you.

'Awareness, not age, leads to wisdom.'
Publilius Syrus, Roman slave and writer (85–43 BCE)

Power words
Clairvoyance, divination, divine, feeling, feminine, intuition, perception, premonition.

Cosmic force influencing you
The High Priestess is linked to the Moon, the source of our emotions and feelings which, when understood, can guide us to clarity. If today is a Full or New Moon, honour it. Full Moons are about completion and celebration, New Moons focus on activation and starting new projects or roles.

Positive action you can take right now
Learn the ritual that we call parting the veil so you can access your inner wisdom.

✦ Press your hands together in front of you and, using deep breaths that pull in energy from your surroundings, visualize the energy moving from your core to your shoulders, down your arms and into your hands.

✦ You may wish to push your hands together with a subtle pulsing pressure as the energy between them builds up.

✦ When you think you are charged with energy, move your hands forwards as if you were pushing your fingertips into the place where two curtains meet.

✦ Pull your hands apart using the same movement you would use to open curtains, thus parting the veil. Look through this portal with your mind's eye. What do you see?

3/THE EMPRESS

The Empress is embracing you. She represents Venus, fertility, Mother Nature. She asks you to start your efforts to make the world a better place from where you live: support your partner, instil your children with strong values, diffuse tensions at work, show respect to your neighbours, contribute to your community. Start at home and radiate outwards. Let the Empress create a warm glow of good will around you.

Daily oracle message
Today is the day that YOU activate your Empress glow! Begin to pour love and kindness into your realm. Starting at your own feet, circle around, going wider and wider, to reach family, friends, neighbours, colleagues and community. Be a beacon of goodwill. Stand tall in this bright light you created. Love attracts love.

Message of encouragement
However bleak things may feel sometimes, you will ALWAYS feel better by doing something good for someone else and reinforcing the loving feeling you have for them. Love grows, it spreads, it's all around. Tap into that vein.

'Spread love everywhere you go. Let no one ever come to you without leaving happier.'
Mother Teresa, Albanian-Indian Catholic nun (1910–97)

Power words
Commitment, devotion, family, hearth, home, love, nature, tenderness.

Cosmic force influencing you
The Empress is linked to Venus, the pleasure-seeking planet of beauty, indulgence, romance and money.

Positive action you can take right now
Be Mother Nature yourself and create an elemental garden to attract the energies of the natural elements to fuel your efforts to spread love and light.

- ✦ **Air:** Bells, chimes, incense.
- ✦ **Fire:** Candles, fairy lights, lanterns, reflectors.
- ✦ **Water:** Clear crystals, fountains, ponds, shells, water plants.
- ✦ **Earth:** Bark, fossils, lichens, mosses, rocks, wild flowers.

You could create this in your own garden, in a window box or on a tray in your home. Caring for the elements will fuel you and help make your home feel harmonious.

4 / THE EMPEROR

The Emperor is your tough-love coach. He is here to train you in seeing and wielding your power, influence and ability to control your destiny by making decisions. American novelist Alice Walker (b. 1944) famously said: *'The most common way people give up their power is by thinking they don't have any.'* Don't be one of those people. The Emperor has got your back.

Daily oracle message
Today is the day that YOU realize the power you wield. Consciously pause when something happens and decide, from a higher, future-self perspective, what your BEST response should be. You are creating personal freedom from being swayed by what you don't control.

Message of encouragement
No one can get into your mind and control you. Your thoughts, feelings, ideas and opinions are yours alone. If you have a fortress mentality about your inner world and discipline yourself to be resolute, determined and persistent inside and out, you will become a true force to be reckoned with. Life will get easier.

*'Mastering others is strength.
Mastering yourself is true power.'*
Lao Tzu, Chinese philosopher and writer (b. 571–531 BCE)

Power words
Dynamism, force, influence, potential, power.

Cosmic force influencing you
The Emperor is linked to Aries, the sign associated with Mars and its ambitious, competitive, passionate vitality.

Positive action you can take right now
This visualization will release your limiting self-beliefs.

+ Close your eyes and take deep breaths. Still your mind. Let your whole body go limp and heavy.

+ Now visualize your fears and doubts. See them all gathering as one ball of dark matter in front of you, spinning and spiking. Experience this representation of everything that is holding you back from your fullest power.

+ Now inhale slowly and deeply. With each inhalation, imagine a bright light shining through you, blasting the dark matter.

+ With each exhalation, visualize this ball of fear getting smaller and smaller. Repeat until this ball of dark matter has evaporated into nothing.

5/ THE HIEROPHANT

The Hierophant is often thought of as a pope or spiritual guru, associated with leadership, mentoring and sometimes rebellion against an old system. There's a deep need in all of us to feel as though we belong to a greater good. In youth, our education and friendships tend to fulfil this territory. In adulthood, we have to find our own 'tribe', our own collective which aligns with our needs, interests or goals. This is what you're figuring out. Be patient.

Daily oracle message
Today is the day that YOU make a stand in favour of something you truly believe in. Join forces with like-minded folk and add your voice, energy, resources or talents to something you wish to uphold, change or support.

Message of encouragement
You can change your allegiances. Opinions, outlook and appetites grow and develop through life and so too will your social circle, interests and memberships. Be hopeful and honest in seeking the collectives you now wish to align with.

'There is strength in numbers, yes, but even more so in collective good will. For those endeavors are supported by mighty forces unseen.'
Richelle E. Goodrich, American author (b. 1968)

Power words
Collaboration, collective, co-operative, fellowship, force, squad, wave.

Cosmic force influencing you
The Hierophant is linked to Taurus, the sign associated with determination, stoicism and analysis.

Positive action you can take right now
Select a role model. This person should have done something or been involved in something you aspire to. Their experience is interesting, resonant and relevant to you right now. They could be in your direct circle already, a step away from it, or even someone famous, either alive or in the past. Make a list of the ways you can learn from them, given their status, through reading, documentaries or podcasts. You may even be able to reach out to them directly through a phone call, letters, social media or even an online or face-to-face interview.

6 / THE LOVERS

Humans are fickle. We want what we can't have. We tear ourselves into pieces trying to resolve conflicting forces within us. *'I can resist everything but temptation,'* British author Oscar Wilde said. The Lovers acknowledges this flaw. Don't judge yourself too harshly in the moment but do challenge yourself to do the right thing in the long run. Decide if this temptation is real, sustained, justified (if so, perhaps it's indicating a change you DO need to make – only you can decide this). Know the consequences, think it through. Prioritize your 'loves' and act accordingly.

Daily oracle message
Today is the day that YOU admit you are tempted by something outside of your realm and you're going to explore this feeling, examine the root cause, consider the consequences, and decide a course of action that is ethical, fair and feasible to enact.

Message of encouragement
We are all complex, fickle and changeable, and we are all visited by temptation (over-eating or spending, laziness, gossiping, feeling jealous, lying or cheating, abusing substances). The measure of your character is how you handle that. Decide what you love most, what you are protecting or striving to keep ... and act that way. Serve a higher force. Distract and displace bad habits. Change the environment. You can resist.

'We gain the strength of the temptation we resist.'
Ralph Waldo Emerson, American essayist (1803–82)

Power words
Authenticity, choices, constancy, dignity, fortitude, patience, truth.

Cosmic force influencing you
The Lovers is linked to Gemini, the sign of the twins and the duality that exists in all humans.

Positive action you can take right now
Four ways to resist a temptation:

+ **Distance:** Remove yourself from the situation.
+ **Distraction:** Distract yourself by doing something else involving, absorbing and rewarding.
+ **Visualization:** Visualize yourself resisting the temptation and reaping the rewards.
+ **Prediction:** Predict the consequences of yielding to scare yourself with what is at stake.

7/THE CHARIOT

A life without purpose is like a ship without a rudder: drifting, aimless. Yet many of us live without a purpose. It can take until you're into middle age, triggered by a life-changing event or two, to really understand just how short and precious life is, to appreciate that you must take control and give your time meaning. Be patient with yourself. This revelation may be years in the making but keep it on your 'back burner' and don't let it fade.

Daily oracle message
Today is the day that YOU hook your wagon to the purpose-seeking chariot! Discover your potential gifts and create a purpose around sharing them with others in this life. Ask for feedback, input, ideas. Review past successes, achievements, childhood passions. Zoom in on what you love doing, and what others love about you, then do more of it.

Message of encouragement
Your purpose in life is simply to share what you're good at. Everyone is different. Your purpose shouldn't look like anyone else's, and certainly not like a corporate or social media-styled mantra. Create your own weird destiny.

'The meaning of life is to find your gift. The purpose of life is to give it away.'
Pablo Picasso, Spanish artist (1881–1973)

Power words
Ambition, aspiration, desire, intent, principle, reason, target, wish.

Cosmic force influencing you
The Chariot is linked to Cancer, the sign of intuition, protectiveness and creativity.

Positive action you can take right now
Think about your eulogy traits (rather than your career or CV skills). Think about what people would say they loved and liked about you, what you were known for, trusted with and what characteristics made people talk about you.

Ask others about their eulogy traits. Consider people you know and respect and what their eulogy traits are. This activity re-focuses your thinking beyond the here and now, the everyday, and the alpha / career self-reflection we so often prioritize. Look at the bigger picture. What legacy do you want to build? How can you invest your time here meaningfully? It can all start here.

8/ STRENGTH

The Strength card comes to you with a message today: value your strength. It has taken a lifetime to get here, and many tests and trials have already been overcome. You are wiser and more powerful than you know. There are depths of courage, determination and resilience within you that you don't even see are there. Whatever you need will rise to the surface to be used. The stronger you are, the easier life becomes. Strength grows when it is used.

Daily oracle message
Today is the day that YOU celebrate how strong you are and do something to prove it to yourself. Be a rock for others and encourage them, too.

Message of encouragement
Strength is not just about brute force, confidence or showy traits that attract attention. Strength can be humble, even silent and unacknowledged. Strength comes from enduring, carrying on, giving meaning to pain, extracting life lessons from hardship. Simply deciding to carry on. You can do that.

'Out of suffering have emerged the strongest souls; the most massive characters are seared with scars.'
Kahlil Gibran, Lebanese-American writer and poet (1883–1931)

Power words
Courage, durability, energy, fortitude, mercy, patience, power, stability, tenacity, vigour, vitality, wisdom.

Cosmic force influencing you
Strength is linked to Leo, the sign of leadership, warrior-like energy and confidence.

Positive action you can take right now
Here are three ways to survive a tough day:

+ **Walk:** Go outside for at least half an hour to clear your mind. Breathe deeply, look up at the sky and regain perspective. This is just a day, a moment, a drop in the ocean of your long life.

+ **Meditate:** Use an app, music, outdoor sounds, a guided recording. Rest your mind.

+ **Journal:** Write down your feelings, fears, hopes, ideas DAILY, or even twice a day. Get it all OUT of your head and ON paper.

9/THE HERMIT

The Hermit is a master of humility, the wisest of all for being at peace with understanding that there's much we don't know, and a lot of what we do think we know is likely to be warped or plain wrong. There is rarely one singular 'truth', and admitting that frees you from ideology, dogma and rigidity. You are a free-flowing entity, ready and eager to learn, be enlightened, change your mind, evolve and seek powerful insights. American rapper Nas (b. 1973) said, 'Read more, learn more, change the globe.'

Daily oracle message
Today is the day that YOU open your mind and see your life and environment as offering a series of lessons. Spot the opportunity to ask a question, seek a different point of view, research the background. Make today (and every day) a series of lessons and learnings that you extract from life and craft within.

Message of encouragement
The Hermit is with you today and whenever you need him. He is your guide to translating external events and happenings into internally grown wisdom, values, opinions and ideas. Let him help you discern the facts, see the root causes, extract a universal truth. We become wise when we look further, broader and deeper.

'Be less curious about people and more curious about ideas.'
Marie Curie, Polish-French physicist (1867–1934)

Power words
Determine, discern, educate, enlighten, illuminate, memorize, prepare, reveal, study.

Cosmic force influencing you
The Hermit is linked to Virgo, the sign of practical expertise, knowledge and self-improvement.

Positive action you can take right now
Stop scrolling and looking at your phone so much today. Social media can be a gallery of lives you aren't living, diets you aren't following, events you're not attending, fun you're not having. Cut yourself a break.

Scroll your own mind instead. Scroll your consciousness for reasons to be grateful to be you, for truths you've learnt about other people, for new ideas you want to experiment with and try, for unanswered questions you want to get to the bottom of.

10/THE WHEEL OF FORTUNE

The only constant in life is change, right? We all live with the Wheel of Fortune and dance a fine line between free will and fate; no one can fully control their destiny, and no one is powerless in their fate either. Occupy this mindset: spin the narrative to a positive slant, embrace change, get comfortable with your own shifts. Notice the synchronistic events that underpin a 'good day' – such as getting a good night's sleep, not doom scrolling – ordinary things. Join the dots, design the right environment, give yourself the best chance of riding the waves.

Daily oracle message
Today is the day that YOU can make something new happen! The Wheel of Fortune is there to be spun whenever you choose. Pick an area you want to change and act. Let the momentum unfold.

Message of encouragement
The 24-hour rule asks you to turn the page every day, no matter what. You can celebrate or commiserate, but tomorrow you turn the page. Tomorrow is a new day. Learn from the past but don't dwell on it. Yesterday is over.

'When we are no longer able to change a situation – we are challenged to change ourselves.'
Viktor E. Frankl, Austrian physicist (1905–97)

Power words
Adjust, change, develop, flow, innovate, modify, pivot, respond, shift, switch, transform.

Cosmic force influencing you
The Wheel of Fortune is linked to Jupiter, the positive planet of abundance, good luck and opportunity.

Positive action you can take right now
If someone asked you to tell them how many red cars you noticed after taking a journey, you'd have no idea because you didn't notice. But if they asked you to look for red cars beforehand, you would notice many more. What we notice becomes our experience, our reality. Today, ask yourself to notice something positive (such as reasons to be grateful, kindness in other people, happy happenings) and keep a tally. Lean in to noticing good stuff and more good stuff will happen! This is you learning to take the wheel, extract the fortune and seek positive energy.

11/ JUSTICE

Justice is a powerful concept and vastly discussed in today's world, and the first step towards being just is finding and following your own moral compass. *'Only a fool lets somebody else tell him who his enemy is,'* said American political activist Assata Shakur (b. 1947). We must remember that justice is NOT revenge. Accept no story at face value without listening for the silenced. Weigh the facts. Research the options. Sleep on situations. Heed your gut instinct. Quiet your ego and let your moral compass guide you in life.

Daily oracle message
Today is the day that YOU decide to be the change you wish to see. Want more fairness, then be fair. Want more kindness, then be kind. Set a good example. Action (even quietly done in private) has more impact than you know.

Message of encouragement
Mistakes and injustices, no matter how accepted, often carry the seeds of their own destruction. The wheels of justice grind slowly, but they do grind. Don't follow the crowd, follow your conscience. Be patient, fair and steadfast.

'Intentionally avoiding the painful details of reality is not a credible excuse for inaction. Some of us know, as we begin to lift the curtain and witness to the world for what it is, our own conscience will begin to demand more of us.'
Cole Arthur Riley, American writer (b. 1992)

Power words
Equity, fairness, honesty, honour, impartiality, integrity, objectivity, principle.

Cosmic force influencing you
Justice is linked to Libra, the sign of analytical thinking, balance and harmony.

Positive action you can take right now
'Freedom under the law' is a basic premise of our society, but how much do you know about the law? What elements of it have you brushed up against, encountered or simply found interesting? Today, read up, listen to a podcast or watch a documentary about an aspect of the law that resonates with you. Unpick how and why this law was crafted. Learn to think like a law-maker. It will help you in smaller matters.

12 / THE HANGED MAN

This character is suspended, in a limbo, swinging in the breeze, and it reflects the fact you've likely hit a blockage and feel frustrated because nothing is moving forwards like you expected it to. Your efforts have not been rewarded. So, stop, rethink the situation, make a new sacrifice, and then let the changed energies work their magic. Allow the Universe to work through you. You need to see this situation from a new angle or perspective to unlock the solution or next step. Let go of what you've been doing or expecting to happen.

Daily oracle message
Today is the day that YOU change your mind. It's not a defeat or a step down. It's growth, change, progression, liberation.

Message of encouragement
Stop banging your head on this brick wall. Stop trying so hard. Surrender, let it be what it is, step back and be peaceful, quiet and still. A change of mind is coming. Welcome it. See this situation as a mystery that you're going to get to the bottom of; there are unseen forces at play that you need to align with.

'Those who cannot change their minds cannot change anything.'
George Bernard Shaw, Irish playwright and critic (1856–1950)

Power words
Discernment, divination, enlightenment, patience, sacrifice, surrender, wait.

Cosmic force influencing you
The Hanged Man is linked to Neptune, the mystical planet of illusion, secret wisdom and mysterious forces.

Positive action you can take right now
Practise projection. Practise the art of putting yourself in someone else's shoes and seeing a certain situation, person or role from their perspective. Make it a fantasy character (Athena!), a role model or celebrity (someone you admire), if you wish. When you can get out of your own ego, mindset and point of view and embrace another, you will accelerate towards finding new, innovative, equitable, effective solutions and resolutions to long-held issues.

13/ DEATH

The Death card indicates not actual death but whispers in your ear that a phase of your life – of outworn and outgrown habits or situations – is ending. You knew it, right? You did. It's time to move on and change. Death will help you end what needs to be ended. Death will help you through that pivot, that transformative episode, that before vs after moment in time. You are ready to revive, rejuvenate, reinvent. A 2.0 version of you is waiting, just up ahead. Take Death's hand and let him lead you there.

Daily oracle message
Today is the day that YOU release an old self, an old way of life, an old pattern that no longer serves you. A 'little death' of your old ways.

Message of encouragement
It's time to let go, bury an old and worn version of you, so that a new model can emerge.

Power words
Conversion, evolution, flames, metamorphosis, overhaul, phoenix, renovation, revolution.

Cosmic force influencing you
Death is linked to Pluto, the intense planet of death, rebirth and transformation.

Positive action you can take right now
Step into your 2.0 version. Make a list of the elements of the identity you wish to adopt and imagine yourself fusing with this identity – how you might look, talk, walk and act. If you're unsure, seek a mentor or confidante to bounce ideas off. Now develop steps that would confirm that you're aligning with your new identity. Think about the things you do, your lifestyle, your work, your social life, where you go. Start making these changes.

Now fuse into that new person, take the steps and act this way, tell people about the changes you're making.

14/ Temperance

A life well lived usually boils down to one thing: moderation. A little bit of everything in moderation, including moderation itself! And yet, all the time life conspires to push to extremes, outliers and tight corners. It's up to us to recognize when this happens and to recalibrate, find the middle ground, come back to a safe and stable position where we feel strong and supported.

Daily oracle message
Today is the day that YOU rebalance the conflicting or competing forces in your life to find the middle ground. Rein it in, step it up, balance the books, prioritize harmony and peace.

Message of encouragement
You can't always control what happens, but you can consciously decide your reaction to it. Once the emotions have risen and fallen, think about your narrative, lesson, adjustments and outlook. Be a work in progress at all times. Go with the flow and adjust as you go.

'And once the storm is over you won't remember how you made it through, how you managed to survive. You won't even be sure, in fact, whether the storm is really over. But one thing is certain. When you come out of the storm you won't be the same person who walked in. That's what this storm's all about.'
Haruki Murakami, Japanese writer (b. 1949)

Power words
Balance, constraint, control, discretion, grounding, harmony, healing, moderation, recovery.

Cosmic force influencing you
Temperance is linked to Sagittarius, the sign of freedom, philosophy and truth.

Positive action you can take right now
Think about and create a set of values that you want to live your life by. It will help you process and respond positively to impacts and extremes in life. For example, health and vitality, love and warmth, learning and growing, achieving and succeeding, creating and inventing, caring and sharing. Pressure-test yourself by assessing a recent stressful event through the lens of your values. How should you best have responded and adjusted to it? How can your values help you put things in perspective when they happen? Create a little framework and process yourself.

15/THE DEVIL

The Devil lives inside you. I think you knew that, right? We all carry our own heaven and hell, and the hell is a place that is reached by paths of least resistance, short cuts, worn bad habits or unhealthy patterns. Just because the results aren't immediately felt doesn't mean consequences aren't coming. Notice when your devil is awake and leading you to a hellish place.

Daily oracle message
Today is the day that YOU exercise conscious self-control, forethought and planning. Remove temptation from your realm. Self-control can run out, so it's better to avoid temptation in the first place rather than try to resist it once it arises.

Message of encouragement
One simple way to unlock your best self is to shape your environment so that your desired behaviour is the path of least resistance. Make your environment a place your inner devil doesn't like.

'Monsters are real, and ghosts are real too. They live inside us, and sometimes, they win.'
Stephen King, American novelist (b. 1947)

Power words
Discipline, endurance, fortitude, liberation, resolve, sobriety, tenacity, willpower.

Cosmic force influencing you
The Devil is linked to Saturn, the tough-talking planet of responsibility, maturity and commitment.

Positive action you can take right now
Talk to, and reason with, your inner devil today.

✦ Close your eyes, take several deep and slow breaths.

✦ Imagine you are sitting on a bench in a peaceful garden. Behind you is the sound of footsteps approaching, and you recognize them as your devil's gait. You know it well, because it has walked beside you many times.

✦ The footsteps get louder and nearer and your devil takes a seat next to you. Turning to face it, you feel no fear, only curiosity and sympathy. It wants to talk. It wants to tell you what it wants, why, and how you can help it find peace.

✦ Show your devil understanding and compassion. Shame cannot survive in the face of true empathy.

✦ What does your demon say? Listen carefully. Be patient, compassionate and receptive to its words.

16 / THE TOWER

Sudden, unexpected changes or revelations are rarely to anyone's liking but the Tower is bringing one your way. Take a deep breath. It serves as a messenger from the Universe, which is using this event, or news, to collapse something in your realm that has long been shaky and unsafe. In short, this is happening for the best. You are being liberated and released from a fading, false or negative situation, commitment, role or relationship. Let the painful moment pass and look ahead to your comeback. Every ending is the embryo of a new beginning.

Daily oracle message
Today is the day that YOU let something leave your life that no longer serves you and welcome the opportunity to rebuild and replace it, now older and wiser.

Message of encouragement
Everything is as everything should be. Even if an event is painful it doesn't mean it's not positive in the long run. This hard moment is but a drop in the ocean of your whole life. Acknowledge the feeling but don't dwell on it. You are being propelled forwards, away from this place. Seek out wisdom, meaning and a life lesson, then move on.

'Life is never made unbearable by circumstances, but only by lack of meaning and purpose.'
Viktor Frankl, Austrian psychiatrist (1905–97)

Power words
Fix, heal, mend, rebuild, rejuvenate, repair, replace, restore.

Cosmic force influencing you
The Tower is linked to Mars, the fiery, combative planet of passion and ambition.

Positive action you can take right now
Read these words whenever you feel it's all too much. The toughest part of any experience is when you feel as though you can't take any more, so if you feel like that now, then chances are you've already reached the worst point. This is the dark before the dawn. You have survived everything you have been through, and you will survive this too. Stay, breathe, heal, and cheer for the person you are becoming. You are a whole future of possibilities.

17 / THE STAR

The Star sprinkles fairy dust and magic all over you and your realm today, specifically bringing you a cosmic 'wish pass' from the Universe, which you can exchange for your heart's desire. Truly, make a dream come true for yourself, gift yourself what you most want. Have faith in your vision, imagine it being real, and make overt, positive steps in its direction. Good fortune and opportunity will swiftly follow.

Daily oracle message
Today is the day that YOU breathe life and hope into a long-held dream or desire. Manifest, make a wish, reach out. The higher you aim, the better the outcome. If you don't feel inspired, then go outside and look up to the sky (day or night). Let your mind roam, see shapes and symbols in clouds and star patterns. Let the cosmos bring you a magical idea today. Look up.

Message of encouragement
Don't discount or disregard your daydreams. Believe in them. They are unique and personal to you, serving as a kind of blueprint to show you what's possible, what's just right for you.

'If you can dream it. You can do it.'
Walt Disney, American entertainment icon (1901–66)

Power words
Ambition, belief, desire, faith, hope, optimism, promise, wish.

Cosmic force influencing you
The Star is linked to Aquarius, the sign of truth, progress and humanity.

Positive action you can take right now
The following herbs can be added to food, drink, aromatherapy blends or homemade toiletries to enhance your wish fulfilment. You could even put dried or fresh mixes into a little cloth bag and keep it with you or under your pillow at night.

- **Love:** Apple, basil, dill, jasmine, lavender, thyme.
- **Wealth:** Allspice, cedar, comfrey, ginger, honeysuckle.
- **Health:** Coriander (cilantro), juniper, knotweed, nutmeg, oak, rue.
- **Happiness:** Catnip, hawthorn, hyacinth, marjoram.

18/THE MOON

The Moon is mysterious. A reflecting versus illuminating entity. There is a side of the Moon that we cannot see from Earth as it remains in shadow – much like our view of other people, maybe even our own whole personality. Accepting that we can't see a lot of what goes on around us is necessary but, equally, knowing when it's time to dig deeper and get to the bottom of something is valuable. Trust your intuition. You know when you're not getting the whole story and you know when you need it.

Daily oracle message
Today is the day that YOU dig, probe, ask, research, validate, double-check and see beyond the façade of a situation. Look deeper. Answer unanswered questions.

Message of encouragement
None of us can see the whole picture. None of us knows what others think, say or do behind our back. All we can do is live our life in tune with our moral compass, values and true desires. When unanswered questions or mysteries arise, put on your detective hat and try to uncover what's going on. Don't suppress difficult information. Bring light to it. Understand it, and then act on it.

'All of us labour in webs spun long before we were born.'
William Faulkner, American novelist (1897–1962)

Power words
Clarify, decipher, decode, divine, determine, illuminate, puzzle, solve, unravel.

Cosmic force influencing you
The Moon is linked to Pisces, the sign of esoteric, psychic and intuitive power.

Positive action you can take right now
You can use this bath to release a burden or worry.

- ✦ Run yourself a magical moonlit bath tonight. Make this something special by lighting candles and using crystals, essential oils, bath salts, rose petals, pampering skincare or fragrant toiletries.
- ✦ Keep the window or blind open so the lunar rays can stream in (without compromising your privacy!).
- ✦ Write down what is troubling you in ink on a scrap of paper and pop it in your bath. When you pull the plug, stay in the bath and feel the water draining away and imagine this weight is dissolving and flowing away from your psyche.
- ✦ Take the scrap of paper and bury it.

19/THE SUN

The Sun is the tarot's most positive card and literally brings warmth, light, possibility, love, joy and vitality into your life, so welcome in fresh energy and smile at the world because it's ready to smile right back.

Daily oracle message
Today is the day that YOU take a step into the life you wish you were living. Apply, pitch, propose, ask, demand, challenge, decide, commit. It all starts with your positive, proactive decisions.

Message of encouragement
You are standing in front of a portal which leads to a new lifestyle, offering everything you want. What's stopping you? We only get one life and our sole task is to live it as well as we can. There's nothing to fear as it all ends the same for each of us. We are all equal and you have a right to take your share of good fortune. Feast on your desires.

'Everything you've ever wanted is on the other side of fear.'
George Addair,
American real-estate developer (1823–99)

Power words
Bloom, energy, force, life, sparkle, spirit, vigour, vitality, zest.

Cosmic force influencing you
The Sun is linked to the literal Sun, the universe's source of heat, light and energy.

Positive action you can take right now
Tap into the magical energy of the Sun today. Simply go outside and find a comfortable spot to bask in the sunlight.

✦ Close your eyes, and imagine a fine green mist rising from the ground and all the living, growing things around you.

✦ Take three slow deep breaths and each time you inhale visualize that mist of vibrant green energy flowing into your lungs and spreading through your body.

✦ As you exhale, release tension and stress.

✦ Open your awareness to the warmth of the sunlight; receive it fully. Let it in and notice what energy it brings to you.

✦ Take as long as you wish to commune with the Sun's energy. When you are finished, take a final three deep breaths and open your eyes.

20/ JUDGEMENT

'Be yourself; everyone else is already taken,' said Oscar Wilde. And he was right. Judgement is a sign that you will receive an epiphany very soon that awakens you as to who you truly are, what you're truly all about, and where, therefore, your niche in this world might lie. Discovering, recognizing, celebrating and using our own unique blend of talent, quirk, insight, experience and strength is the key to a contented, fulfilling life. This is the path to purpose. You are on it!

Daily oracle message
Today is the day that YOU stop looking around and outside yourself, comparing yourself to others with an envious or self-recriminating gaze, and start to see who you are in all your glory. Know thyself, know thy opportunity.

Message of encouragement
It's time to awaken the real you, the true personality, the inner maverick and one-off who has shape-shifted and compromised to suit others and fit in. This might be the greatest wake-up call of your whole life.

'The world will ask you who you are, and if you don't know, the world will tell you.'
Carl Jung, Swiss psychiatrist and psychoanalyst (1875–1961)

Power words
Discovery, epiphany, eye-opener, inspiration, lightning bolt, revelation, unearthing.

Cosmic force influencing you
Judgement is linked to Pluto, the intense planet of rebirth, reinvention and inner wisdom.

Positive action you can take right now
Unleash your inner voice.

+ Put a drop of lavender essential oil (oil of truth and communication) on your palms and rub them together.

+ Inhale deeply over your cupped hands for three breaths.

+ Use a crystal associated with honesty and communication (amazonite, blue lace agate, lapis lazuli). Hold the crystal at your throat while counting your inhale for four seconds and your exhale for four seconds.

+ Repeat an affirmation that resonates, such as, 'I am expressing my unique personality.'

21 / THE WORLD

The major arcana's final card reminds us of life cycles. Things are born, grow, fade and die. Nature moves in cycles and seasons, ebb and flow, a continual circle of beginnings and endings. So too does your own life. Everything is at a different stage. Feel the truth of this. Learn to juggle the different stages and phases of the multiple elements and aspects of your life. Every achievement is a signal to start a new journey. Every loss or failure is an invitation to transform. Never stop growing, adjusting, changing and moving.

Daily oracle message
Today is the day that YOU celebrate your successes, take wisdom from your failures, put everything in your realm into perspective, and discern where you are drawing towards an ending and where you are creating a new beginning. Live in full flow.

Message of encouragement
And the wheel keeps on turning, there is no endpoint. All rivers run to the sea, but the sea is not full. Life goes on, the Sun rises the morning after, a new dawn always awaits us. Take comfort that wherever you're at, there is always more left to enjoy, achieve, celebrate, appreciate and strive for. Your story never ends.

'Large angels take a long time unfolding their wings, but when they do, soar out of sight.'
David Brooks, American author and journalist (b. 1961)

Power words
Advancing, evolution, expansion, flowering, flowing, growth, progression, unfolding.

Cosmic force influencing you
The World is linked to Saturn, the uncompromising planet of duty, commitment and work.

Positive action you can take right now
We only live with one person for our whole life – ourself. And to do so means attending a thousand metaphorical 'funerals' of the person we used to be, the person we're too exhausted to be or grew out of. Hold a little farewell celebration for your past selves today. Appreciate and eulogize how they did what they did at the time for the best, what you loved about them. And then lay to rest the things about them that have faded. Get comfortable seeing yourself as a work in progress, a microcosm of mini life cycles and personal 'deaths', ever evolving.

The Suit of Coins
60

The Coins suit is linked to the element of Earth and is concerned with practical, material fundamentals in life like health, wealth, work and home.

The Suit of Cups
74

The Cups suit is linked to the element of Water and is concerned with emotional, spiritual and relationship-linked matters. Insights about family, friends, lovers and feelings dwell in this suit.

The Suit of Swords
88

The Swords suit is linked to the element of Air and is concerned with intellectual, cerebral, opinion-based matters of the mind. Swords cards often reveal conflicts, ideas and decisions.

The Suit of Wands
102

The Wands suit is linked to the element of Fire and is concerned with inspiring, passion-led, and purposeful activity – what gets us going. Wands cards often points to actions around travel, healthy lifestyle, creativity or education.

THE MINOR ARCANA

These are the equivalent to a standard pack of cards,
Ace to Ten, then Page, Knight, Queen and King
in each of four suits: Cups, Coins, Wands and Swords.

ACE OF COINS

Aces are new beginnings and today marks one for you. It will be something linked to health, wealth, work or home, and within your circle of influence. This is a long-term investment, at least one year. It is something you take baby steps on each day and, over time, they all add up to a giant leap.

Daily oracle message
Today is the day that YOU figure out the one thing you can do today that makes tomorrow easier (regarding health, wealth, work or home). Do it. Repeat. No matter how tired you feel or difficult life is, you can always do one thing to make tomorrow better.

Message of encouragement
Fear of failure is highest when you're looking at the ultimate destination. To reduce fear, close the gap. Focus on the smallest action to move you forwards. This is within your gift, this you can do, and do well.

'The willingness to accept responsibility for one's own life is the source from which self-respect springs.'
Joan Didion, American writer and journalist (1934–2021)

Power words
Grow, invest, plant, raise, seed, sow, start.

Cosmic force influencing you
The Earth element is the most powerful motivator throughout the suit of Coins. Connect to Earth today by planting your bare feet in grass or soil, or hugging a tree. Earth indicates springtime and the signs of Taurus, Virgo and Capricorn.

Positive action you can take right now
Connect to Earth today by planting something! It could be a fruit, vegetable or flower in whatever outdoor or window sill space you possess. If outside space is non-existent, introduce an indoor plant to your home, or even scatter a packet of seeds on a piece of wild grass or plant a few bulbs on land near to your house. See this act as a reflection of your ability to create, invent, activate and contribute new life, energy and possibility to your corner of the planet. Be a gardener – physically and mentally. Sow today to reap tomorrow.

TWO OF COINS

You can't buy, borrow or obtain abundance ... you tune in to it. It's a vibration, a wave, a flow, and you can align simply by opening your mind to the idea that you will say 'yes' and welcome whatever comes your way today. The more you do, the more you find you can do. Variety keeps us sharp, vital and grounded. The world is vast and interesting; you can never 'finish' it. Open up to it.

Daily oracle message
Today is the day that YOU say 'yes' to everything, that you embrace new energy and ideas, that you sign up, apply, join in and contribute. Fill your world with new news.

Message of encouragement
You don't need good health, money, charm, beauty or talent to enjoy your life. A good life well lived starts with having interests, passions, hobbies, pastimes and themes which please you and you immerse yourself in. Don't limit yourself here. Grab as much of what interests you as possible.

'A man who limits his interests limits his life.'
Vincent Price, American actor (1911–93)

Power words
Affluence, bounty, myriad, plenty, profusion, prosperity, riches.

Cosmic force influencing you
The Earth element is the most powerful motivator throughout the suit of Coins. Connect to Earth today by planting your bare feet in grass or soil, or hugging a tree. Earth indicates springtime and the signs of Taurus, Virgo and Capricorn.

Positive action you can take right now
Be curious today. Choose an activity to connect with the Earth. Google local events, classes or exhibitions – preferably outdoors – happening this weekend and pick one to try. Find out where your local library is and pick a day to visit. Or book an outing within the coming three weeks and write a list of places you are going to visit this year.

THE MINOR ARCANA

THREE OF COINS

You don't realize how admired and respected you are, you know. The way you've carried yourself has drawn attention and esteem. You have acted in good faith, with integrity, worked hard, borne the burdens and been a humble hero. Now, others are in a position to give you an opportunity to rise up, one which you have wholeheartedly earned. It's time to get what you're owed.

Daily oracle message
Today is the day that YOU put yourself overtly in front of people with influence to showcase your successes, achievements and talents. It's time to get what you deserve.

Message of encouragement
Good character is priceless and will work for you, silently, consistently, in the background, like your greatest ally. People value integrity and diligence above all. Trust is the foundation of all bonds. Know your worth, protect your good character, and let it work for you.

'This is the mark of a really admirable man: steadfastness in the face of trouble. To be one's self, and unafraid whether right or wrong, is more admirable than the easy cowardice of surrender to conformity.'
Ludwig Van Beethoven, German composer (1770–1827)

Power words
Admiration, dignity, esteem, integrity, respect, self-worth, value.

Cosmic force influencing you
The Earth element is the most powerful motivator throughout the suit of Coins. Connect to Earth today by planting your bare feet in grass or soil, or hugging a tree. Earth indicates springtime and the signs of Taurus, Virgo and Capricorn.

Positive action you can take right now
Wear green today – as an outfit, accessory or accent. Green is a powerful colour of luck, growth, youth and beauty. It is an 'attractor' colour and will help to accelerate the opportunities and invitations that are heading your way because of the admiration others carry for you and your character. Amplify and enhance your good fortune and serendipitous luck today by wearing and using green energy.

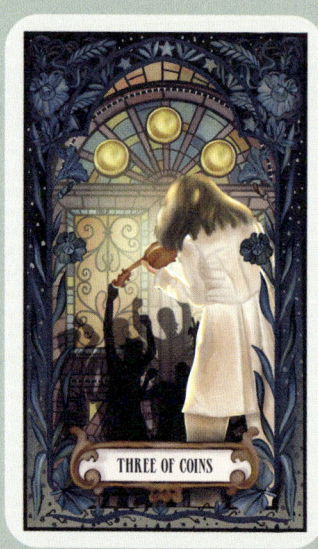

FOUR OF COINS

We all get into ruts, grooves, patterns, habits, routines. Mostly it's necessary and useful to have a structure to our lives, but sometimes these routines and habits outlive their original purpose, and then they feel constraining or stale. We feel stuck, but that is not the reality. We are free to move, grow and redesign whenever we wish. It all starts mentally, deep within, and radiates outwards.

Daily oracle message
Today is the day that YOU refresh and renew your activities, outlook, relationships, social life, priorities and ideas. Be different. Seek newness.

Message of encouragement
Your recent frustration is simply a symptom of being ready for a new structure and routine. See it as such and move into 'action phase'. Re-discover your gratitude for what you have ... and value it. Notice what's stale, outdated or frustrating ... and change it. Do a 'future you' a service.

Power words
Affluence, bounty, myriad, plenty, profusion, prosperity, riches.

Positive action you can take right now
Clear your chakras – your physical and spiritual energy centres – and get your body's subtle energy flowing again.

- Breathe into your root chakra at the base of your spine, where the weight of your body rests, and feel yourself grounding.
- Next, move your awareness to your sacral chakra, just below your naval, and visualize a bright light encircling it; know that you are in control of designing your own life.
- Move up to your solar plexus chakra, your personal power source, and breathe in red, passionate fire, spurring you to ignite a new goal.
- Shift towards your heart chakra and imagine it pulsing with green light; tell yourself you are loved and free to express love.
- Bring your awareness to your third eye, in the middle of your forehead, where your psychic ability resides, and breathe in deep purple energy, which unlocks a new vision. Remain in this meditation until your breathing slows and you feel aligned and strong.

FIVE OF COINS

Every one of us goes through bad times; it's a part of our human experience and there's no ducking it. The trick? To come out of your sad times wiser, not wounded. Don't be a person who internalizes pain, nursing and protecting it until you project it on to others. Use your pain as a lesson, to teach and guide you. Talk about it, share experiences, ask for help. You are connected to others through shared pain.

Daily oracle message
Today is the day that YOU breathe out and release anxiety and regret, and breathe in healing and acceptance. Talk about your painful experiences, write about them, release them to the Universe. Process and move to the next step.

Message of encouragement
You WILL come through this. It's just a moment, it too shall pass. You may come out the other side a little different, older and wiser, shrewder and more compassionate. That's all good. Every darkness has a silver lining.

'If you want the rainbow,
you gotta put up with the rain.'
Dolly Parton, American singer–songwriter (b. 1946)

Power words
Alleviate, heal, mend, rebuild, reconcile, renew, renovate, restore, revive.

Cosmic force influencing you
The Earth element is the most powerful motivator throughout the suit of Coins. Connect to Earth today by planting your bare feet in grass or soil, or hugging a tree. Earth indicates springtime and the signs of Taurus, Virgo and Capricorn.

Positive action you can take right now
Heal your heart space.

Rub a lotion, diluted essential oil or favourite fragrance into your palms and massage your hands together. Healing oils include rose, geranium, patchouli, lavender, ylang ylang and lemon.

✦ Cup your hands over your nose and inhale gently. Close your eyes and imagine this fragrance has healing, soothing, calming power.

✦ Place your hands over your heart and breathe the healing spirit into your heart space. Let it swirl and cocoon your heart and work its magical healing essence through your pain and strife.

SIX OF COINS

Karma is always watching, you know, taking a note of your generosity, helpfulness and kindness. Without attaching yourself to the outcome, share and spread as many kind acts as you possibly can. You will never fully know the impact you make, but you can bet it's positive. Set an example. One apparently trivial but kind action alone may help someone realize how kindness exists and they will remember that for years to come.

Daily oracle message
Today is the day that YOU will do good in a world where a minority is trying to spread havoc. Start the day clean, bright, kind and positive.

Message of encouragement
People rarely remember what you did, said or wore (yet these are the things we obsess over), but they do remember how you made them feel. You can make that difference any time you choose. Be a person who makes others feel good.

'Try not to become a man of success. Rather become a man of value.'
Albert Einstein, German theoretical physicist (1879–1955)

Power words
Patience, courtesy, decency, gentleness, good will, hospitality, sympathy.

Cosmic force influencing you
The Earth element is the most powerful motivator throughout the suit of Coins. Connect to Earth today by planting your bare feet in grass or soil, or hugging a tree. Earth indicates springtime and the signs of Taurus, Virgo and Capricorn.

Positive action you can take right now
It's time to fill your day with kindness. Here are some ideas.

✦ Tell someone that you are proud of them.

✦ Offer to do some voluntary work in your local community, have a clear out and take items to a charity shop, make and send a care package to someone who needs it. Pick up some rubbish lying around in the street.

✦ Get to know the new staff member, offer a listening ear to someone who is having a bad day or have a chat with someone who is homeless.

✦ Let someone jump the queue.

THE MINOR ARCANA

SEVEN OF COINS

Never feel like you're stuck with something that no longer works or serves you, no matter how long it has been a fixture in your life. You can change overnight. You might not be able to totally reinvent your reality or destination, but you can change your direction quickly. We are continually evolving, renewing, shedding and growing. Be proactive and dynamic in this process – forge your own pathway, chart the course, follow the compass you've calibrated.

Daily oracle message
Today is the day that YOU admit what's no longer serving you and give yourself permission to release it and move ahead to a new destination.

Message of encouragement
You have more power in your own destiny than you realize, and by flexing those muscles you will awaken this truth within and feel more confident about manifesting, redesigning and creating your dream life. Start now.

'Always remember, your focus determines your reality.'
George Lucas, American film-maker and philanthropist and creator of the Star Wars and Indiana Jones franchises (b. 1944)

Power words
Evolution, expansion, growth, progression, transformation, unfolding.

Cosmic force influencing you
The Earth element is the most powerful motivator throughout the suit of Coins. Connect to Earth today by planting your bare feet in grass or soil, or hugging a tree. Earth indicates springtime and the signs of Taurus, Virgo and Capricorn.

Positive action you can take right now
Although it seems a small step, clearing out and re-organizing your wardrobe and outfits is a fast-track way to change your outlook, sense of possibility and appetite to evolve personally in life. Throw out what you don't wear or no longer like. Clear the decks a little. Then, pick out certain items that you love and feel drawn to. Take them one by one, and create an outfit around each favourite piece. Bring in accessories, scarves, jewellery, even fragrance. Create mini identities and costumes on hangers, ready for you to dive in and pick out each day.

EIGHT OF COINS

Sometimes you have to be the hardest worker in the room, even at times when you don't feel like it, don't want to carry on, or doubt you're going to be rewarded. Sometimes you have to push on regardless. Karma rewards such endeavour. This card is in your realm today because the Universe doesn't want you to quit. Karma is watching. The task right now is to just keep going. Rewards are waiting.

Daily oracle message
Today is the day that YOU will push on, no matter how tired or bored or frustrated you feel. Simply put one foot in front of the other and keep going.

Message of encouragement
You are going to enjoy a breakthrough very soon. If you keep on this course, then the way will get easier. Success is coming. The hard work you put in now will be paid back handsomely.

'The only place where success comes before work is in the dictionary.'
Vidal Sassoon, British hairstylist and businessman (1928–2012)

Power words
Aim, effort, endeavour, enterprise, venture.

Cosmic force influencing you
The Earth element is the most powerful motivator throughout the suit of Coins. Connect to Earth today by planting your bare feet in grass or soil, or hugging a tree. Earth indicates springtime and the signs of Taurus, Virgo and Capricorn.

Positive action you can take right now
Refuel by connecting to the Earth element via trees – talk to them, meditate among them or hug them.

- Find a place outdoors with lots of trees (or a garden, even a house plant, or a video of trees).
- Sit or lie down amongst them and centre yourself by taking a few deep breaths.
- Let your mind's eye wander and connect with the spirit of the trees. Let their trunks be a lesson that you are strong and grounded to Earth. Let your connection with the Earth heal and replenish you. Visualize vibrant green, soothing energy from the trees swirling around you, inhale it deeply, let it pass through your whole body, cleansing and refreshing.

THE MINOR ARCANA

NINE OF COINS

In life, we advance and mature, and our desires, priorities and values change with us. Most people go on a journey towards material security or wealth and then, at a certain point, start to desire a deeper, more spiritual or humane reason for their efforts. You are at that stage. You are thinking about how you align these two desires, how you best enjoy what you do for a living, how you start to build a legacy, how you might create a 'forever home', what kind of preventative and proactive steps for your long-term health you can take now.

Cosmic force influencing you
The Earth element is the most powerful motivator throughout the suit of Coins. Connect to Earth today by planting your bare feet in grass or soil, or hugging a tree. Earth indicates springtime and the signs of Taurus, Virgo and Capricorn.

Positive action you can take right now
Think about the certain, known and likely future outcomes and scenarios coming up in your life (children, retirement, health needs, home improvements, career milestones, and so on). Based on what you already know about your likely future, what steps can you start taking now to make those things as easy, accessible, fulfilling and rewarding as possible. Preparation, preparation, preparation. Pretend you are a (highly paid!) consultant advising on your lifestyle, finances, habits and relationships. What advice would an external voice give?

Daily oracle message
Today is the day that YOU look ahead and build a life that works for a 'future you' and is about self-improvement, personal fulfilment and legacy.

Message of encouragement
You are already far stronger, wiser and more experienced than you give yourself credit for. You have completed many stages and levels in life already, and have reached a stage you can now set your own stages and levels. Be resolute and hopeful.

Power words
Advance, cultivate, enhance, progress, refine, skyrocket, upgrade.

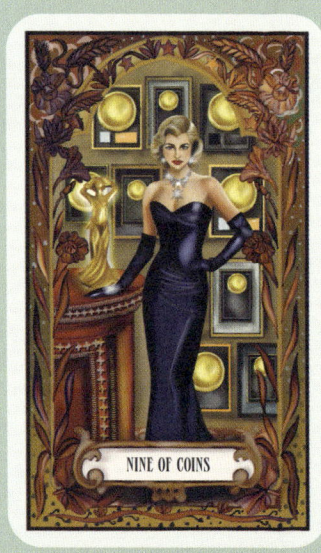

Ten of Coins

Our lives are short. We have already spent billions of years 'dead' before we had life breathed into us. Earth existed long before us and will last long after, but your window of opportunity is here, now, in this present world and set of circumstances. Your job is to figure certain things out: How can you best serve? What is it that needs repair? What tasks are waiting to be performed? Slot yourself into a genuine need in this lifetime and your life will be lived well. Don't seek material gain as an end in itself. Seek a purpose. Build from where you are.

Daily oracle message
Today is the day that YOU count your blessings for a life well lived so far. From here, you can add even more value and positivity to the world. How can you best serve?

Message of encouragement
You have come a long way and achieved a great deal of what you set out to do. Appreciate this journey, your lessons, successes and values. Now is the day to embed deeper meaning and legacy-building purpose into your work, home, wealth and future.

'At what points do my talents and deep gladness meet the world's deep need?'
Frederick Buechner, American author and theologian (1926–2022)

Power words
Employment, legacy, sacrifice, service, usefulness, utility.

Cosmic force influencing you
The Earth element is the most powerful motivator throughout the suit of Coins. Connect to Earth today by planting your bare feet in grass or soil, or hugging a tree. Earth indicates springtime and the signs of Taurus, Virgo and Capricorn.

Positive action you can take right now
Embark on a series of repairs and fixes in and around your home. What's broken, missing, dirty, ill-kept, unloved or messy? Start by improving your immediate surroundings and taking an inventory of the odd jobs that need doing this week and month ahead. Do as much as you can yourself. This not only improves your home but instils a mindset of can-do and positive improvement that you will take out into the wider world with you.

THE MINOR ARCANA

PAGE OF COINS

You are on a quest for wisdom and knowledge, about to enter a phase of learning potentially geared towards your career pathway but maybe for personal development or even just fun. The Page of Coins is a perennial student. There is always something new to learn, absorb, pick up or use. What we put into our brain and skill-set is rarely wasted. Everything is stimulus, everything has value. Seek to learn so you can progress in life.

Daily oracle message
Today is the day that YOU research and consider what skills, talents or practices would be useful to you in the future and how you can acquire them.

Message of encouragement
Adopting the perspective that life is a learning curve, a process of trial and error, a series of lessons, can help to alleviate the pressure and appetite for perfection or always being right first time. Simply live and learn. Follow your interests, appreciating every experience as valuable.

Power words
Discipline, education, information, learning, scholarship, study.

Cosmic force influencing you
The Earth element is the most powerful motivator throughout the suit of Coins. Connect to Earth today by planting your bare feet in grass or soil, or hugging a tree. Earth indicates springtime and the signs of Taurus, Virgo and Capricorn.

Positive action you can take right now
The topics or skills that interest us the most are often implanted in childhood. What we enjoyed doing as kids never really leaves us; it represents our authentic self. You can reconnect to this quite simply.

- Place a few drops of diluted ylang ylang oil on your palms, rubbing your hands together.
- Place them over your nose and mouth and inhale deeply. As you breathe in, imagine the world around you falling away and the years rolling back to the time you were nine or ten years old.
- What books did you most enjoy reading? What classes did you look forward to? What extra-curricular activities did you participate in?

PAGE OF COINS

KNIGHT OF COINS

Take care of the pennies and the pounds will look after themselves. Attention to detail on practical matters always pays off. This Knight is very diligent, hardworking, determined and focused. He enters your realm to help you tackle a period of hard work and perseverance. You need him as your ally and will come to rely on his shrewdness and never-give-up mentality. Keep him close. Talk to him about what is worrying you. Ask for help in taking action to face and overcome your problems.

Daily oracle message
Today is the day that YOU focus on realistic, practical, tangible steps in your material realm: health, wealth, work and home. Get active.

Message of encouragement
Life has already taught you some hard truths. Be wise, not wounded. Be shrewd about using your valuable (even negative) experience to pressure-test your future goals and build life-proofed plans and strategies.

'The roots of education are bitter but the fruit is sweet.'
Aristotle, Greek philosopher (384–322 BCE)

Power words
Business-like, constructive, down-to-earth, efficient, feasible, functional, pragmatic, rational.

Cosmic force influencing you
The Earth element is the most powerful motivator throughout the suit of Coins. Connect to Earth today by planting your bare feet in grass or soil, or hugging a tree. Earth indicates springtime and the signs of Taurus, Virgo and Capricorn.

Positive action you can take right now
Many magical rituals rely on the element of Earth and the Knight of Coins is the embodiment of Earth power. Start to collect literal earth – such as soil, grass, pebbles, rocks, moss – from key places in your realm – your home, work, landscape, childhood haunts, special places – and mix it with the earth in your garden, window boxes or indoor plants. See this as a mindful ritual to create a solid, secure, magically charged foundation. See your home as a place where you can refuel and recharge and make your practical plans for living your best life.

THE MINOR ARCANA

Queen of Coins

There comes a moment in a person's development when they transition from being the one who asks all the questions (child mode) to becoming the one who has to find the answers (adult mode). The Queen of Coins represents that moment, that progression, that scary leap from apprentice to master, child to adult, follower to leader. Heady heights, but you can do this. This moment wouldn't have come if you couldn't. Unseen forces have decided you are ready.

Daily oracle message
Today is the day that YOU step up and take the lead, maybe for the first time in this area of your life. Take control, answer the unanswered questions, accept responsibility for what happens and forge ahead to the best of your ability.

Message of encouragement
Nobody ever feels truly ready to take a big responsibility, be it becoming a parent, buying a house, taking a promotion at work or investing in something new. Nobody gets a guarantee. You do your research, summon your courage and step forwards anyway. A person who is fearless can never be courageous so don't worry if you feel afraid.

'You are only worthy of what you prove yourself to be.'
Alice Hoffman, American novelist (b. 1952)

Power words
Control, courage, ownership, respect, responsibility.

Cosmic force influencing you
The Earth element is the most powerful motivator throughout the suit of Coins. Connect to Earth today by planting your bare feet in grass or soil, or hugging a tree. Earth indicates springtime and the signs of Taurus, Virgo and Capricorn.

Positive action you can take right now
Finding the place where you are meant to be a leader, to be responsible, can be a life's work. You can, however, accelerate that process by analyzing what you're good at and truly enjoy doing, and then matching that to what you see as being needed in your environment and what roles that leads into. Keep this a 'live' analysis in your journal or on your phone. Jot down ideas, insights and observations. Always look for your niche, your potential ideal position, where you can serve, lead and become a monarch.

KING OF COINS

You've made it. You are a king in your realm. You are the one others admire, respect (maybe envy) and lean on for guidance, reassurance, support and approval. Spiderman creator Stan Lee said, *'With great power comes great responsibility.'* This could be aimed at all wannabe superheroes. Power is not a shield but a burden. Its use should be for a cause and for the greater good.

Daily oracle message
Today is the day that YOU use your power, wisely, cautiously, judiciously, but used nonetheless. You have come so far, learnt so much, proved a great deal and surmounted many obstacles. Now is the time to use your power to build, bed down, share and create a legacy.

Message of encouragement
Step into your power. Act the way you would if you knew you couldn't fail. Pursue the highest ideal or ambition you can imagine. You are ready, it is time; this is your life and you're in charge.

'The question isn't who is going to let me; it's who is going to stop me.'
Ayn Rand, author and philosopher (1905–82)

Power words
Dynamism, gift, influence, legacy, potential, power, skill.

Cosmic force influencing you
The Earth element is the most powerful motivator throughout the suit of Coins. Connect to Earth today by planting your bare feet in grass or soil, or hugging a tree. Earth indicates springtime and the signs of Taurus, Virgo and Capricorn.

Positive action you can take right now
Honour your ancestors. You stand now on this Earth as the embodiment, the product, the end game of all the bloodline that has preceded you. Bask in that feeling, that powerful unseen fellowship standing silently at your shoulder, urging you onwards. Perform a simple action that acknowledges their presence – be it wearing a token heirloom, picking flowers, lighting a candle, visiting a grave, researching your family tree or talking to elderly relatives and asking for their advice.

THE MINOR ARCANA

ACE OF CUPS

Aces are new beginnings and today marks one for you – something inspiring, heartfelt and emotive. This new beginning is linked to your heart's highest energy and hopes, so potentially a new romance, deep friendship, family reunion, birth, new pet or creative role or project. Ask for and aspire to 'birth' something into your life that warms your very heart and soul. Fall in love.

Daily oracle message
Today is the day that YOU smile at the world, knowing it will smile back at you. Reach out, connect, introduce yourself, offer help, say hello, make the effort. Feel your powers of attraction flowing.

Message of encouragement
There is no age limit or restriction on our ability to forge new relationships and bonds with people all through our lives. We are social animals so it comes naturally. You can always find new friends, allies and suitors. You are part of a wider community.

'As we journey through life, we all hope for friendship and camaraderie. Those whom we encounter on the way make all the difference; true friends are worth their weight in gold.'
J.R.R Tolkien, British author (1892–1973)

Power words
Attract, captivate, engage, entice, fascinate, magnetize.

Cosmic force influencing you
The Water element is aligned with the suit of Cups. Connect to Water today by drinking iced, fresh water from a blue glass, having a relaxing bath, or walking beside a river or lake. Water indicates summertime and the signs of Pisces, Cancer and Scorpio.

Positive action you can take right now
Wear red or pink to attract romantic, loving, nurturing, passionate energy into your realm today, be that a piece of clothing, accessory, scarf, piece of jewellery – or even nail polish or lipstick! Red is bold and inviting. It has power as a magnetizing colour. Rubies, carnelian, rose quartz and rhodochrosite are all love-promoting crystals you can wear, carry or place around you.

THE MINOR ARCANA

TWO OF CUPS

Fledgling relationships are forming and taking shape – nurture them. The potential is there to build new private kingdoms with others. Whether they are built on romantic, friendly, creative or practical foundations, mutual trust, support, understanding and compromise are vital. Don't think of yourselves as two separate entities vying for control, but as two entities serving a higher force – the relationship itself.

Daily oracle message
Today is the day that YOU invest in a budding relationship, a creative collaboration with promise, a new friendship, or just a moment of emotional self-awareness.

Message of encouragement
There is a lid for every jar! We all have the ability to connect in unique ways with others and create particular chemistries and potential futures. No two partnerships are the same. No one understands the true nature of a relationship except for those experiencing it. Build, nurture and prioritize positive relationships.

'I can do things you cannot, you can do things I cannot; together we can do great things.'
Mother Teresa, Albanian-Indian Catholic nun (1910–97)

Power words
Affinity, agreement, amity, empathy, fit, sympathy.

Positive action you can take right now
Hold a truth session. Sit opposite each other with a timer. Each person gets 20 minutes to speak and share, whilst the other is not allowed to interrupt, only give their full attention. The listener's objective is to see the other for who they truly are, beyond their own expectations and needs, without judgement, blame or projection.

Then swap. When it is your turn to speak, speak your truth about all the things in your heart, those that weigh on you. Tell the truth about how you feel, what you experience, what you need and want and hope for. Agree to let the information you've heard be absorbed. Ask questions compassionately if any arise.

THE MINOR ARCANA

THREE OF CUPS

Life is not always easy, but you can't wait for things to be better / perfect / secure until you let yourself have fun. Have fun every damn day! Seek the pleasure, the humour, the light-hearted perspective, the loving person, the happy moments. Make your own fun, make your own magic, make your own mood higher and brighter and life will bring you things to enjoy. Be a beacon of good fun and happiness, and you will receive more of both.

Daily oracle message
Today is the day that YOU do what makes you happy. Gravitate towards people you love and like and do things together. This creates loving bonds and happy memories. Be joyful.

Message of encouragement
Life is short. We are here for a good time versus a long time. Life is for living, getting busy, having a go, exploring, building great friendships, partnerships and families. Don't save your favourite things for 'best'. Wear them, do them, say them, be them TODAY.

'We must find time to stop and thank the people who make a difference in our lives.'
John F. Kennedy, American President (1917–63)

Power words
Amusement, bliss, buzz, comfort, enjoyment, fun, pleasure.

Cosmic force influencing you
The Water element is aligned with the suit of Cups. Connect to Water today by drinking iced, fresh water from a blue glass, having a relaxing bath, or walking beside a river or lake. Water indicates summertime and the signs of Pisces, Cancer and Scorpio.

Positive action you can take right now
Focus on your friendships today. Do something positive for every one of your pals, be it a kind or complimentary message to them, a gift, an offer of help or practical assistance on something they've got going on, or arranging a beautiful get-together, dinner, day out or social event. Seek to personalize your communication with each friend, letting them know what you love about them, telling them how you best enjoy spending time with them, saying thank you for what they have done for you over the months or years you've known them. Make their day!

THE MINOR ARCANA

FOUR OF CUPS

So often we focus on what we lack, struggle with, wish for but don't have, envy or are striving to achieve. We overthink the 'big moments' (promotions or moving into a new house, for example) and forget that life is lived in the moment, the accumulation of tiny moments that add up to your real pleasure in your life. Noticing what you already have and being grateful for it, celebrating it, using it, relying on it ... that is what will bring you immediate gratitude and contentment.

Daily oracle message
Today is the day that YOU look at what is already right under your nose and say thank you for it. Focus, today, on everything you already have and appreciate your gifts, strengths, advantages and blessings.

Message of encouragement
Happiness is not found 'out there'; it is found within your own heart and mind. Peace, acceptance, gratitude and pleasure are waiting for you in what you already have and already are. You can't be anything you want, but you CAN be everything you are. Celebrate that.

'The power of finding beauty in the humblest things makes home happy and life lovely.'
Louisa May Alcott, American novelist (1832–88)

Power words
Appreciate, grace, gratefulness, praise, thankfulness.

Positive action you can take right now
Much of our life experience depends on what we focus on. The following questions, asked of yourself first thing (write them up and pop them next to your bedside or on your bathroom mirror) will help you start the day right!

✦ What am I happy about in my life right now?

✦ What am I excited about in my life right now?

✦ What am I proud about in my life right now?

✦ What am I grateful about in my life right now?

✦ What am I enjoying most about my life right now?

THE MINOR ARCANA

FIVE OF CUPS

Some emotions are 'sticky' and cling to us and, though we'd love to release them, they emerge at 4am, in the liminal time between night and day, to torture our psyche with shame, guilt, anger, envy, sorrow. We are all haunted by our pasts. No one is a saint, just as no one is altogether a sinner.

Daily oracle message
Today is the day that YOU recognize that shame doesn't serve you, so forgive yourself. Start there and then forgive others. Spread the compassion. Don't let negativity 'stick' to your psyche. Look ahead, not back. Make today all about healing old wounds.

Message of encouragement
Whatever loss or turmoil you've endured, it is a drop in the ocean of your whole life story. Don't cling to it, let it go. Don't stare at the past or that is the direction you will head in.

'In three words I can sum up everything I've learned about life: it goes on.'
Robert Frost, American poet (1874–1963)

Power words
Heal, reconcile, rehabilitate, rejuvenate, settle, soothe.

Cosmic force influencing you
The Water element is aligned with the suit of Cups. Connect to Water today by drinking iced, fresh water from a blue glass, having a relaxing bath, or walking beside a river or lake. Water indicates summertime and the signs of Pisces, Cancer and Scorpio.

Positive action you can take right now
Fill yourself with light to banish the 'sticky' emotions you wish to release.

- Take three deep breaths and, with each, imagine yourself drawing in white, bright light through your nose.
- After the third breath, breathe normally, and enjoy the sensation of being filled with light. Notice how it makes you feel physically and emotionally.
- Allow the light to glow and grow outside your body, into your aura.
- Imagine now that the light in your aura is sparkling as it cleanses and purifies any negative energy trapped there.
- When you feel cleansed, take a final deep breath for emphasis and allow the visualization to fade.

SIX OF CUPS

Affectionate nostalgia is a powerful force. I have seen people in dire straits, or even nearing the end of their life, find great comfort and happiness by revisiting their happiest memories, reliving those times. The past is always with us so why not focus and amplify the best moments. Cherish nostalgia, embrace the love and joyfulness in memories. Connect to your inner child (they are never far away and always ready to play). Remember who you were, what you loved doing, what made you happy. It's likely these things still remain true. Reinvent them.

Daily oracle message
Today is the day that YOU invite your inner child to bring you gifts from your past that you had forgotten. Lost places, activities, hobbies, music, scent, games, fun times, friends, family members and events that were joyful.

Message of encouragement
Pay attention to your inner child, to healing them, to nurturing their needs and desires, and to bringing what they loved doing back into your present realm. This is something each of us can do for ourselves freely and rapidly. Your child is always there waiting for your care and attention.

'It sounds corny, but I've promised my inner child that never again will I ever abandon myself for anything or anyone else again.'
Wynonna Judd, American singer (b. 1964)

Power words
Longing, nostalgia, reminiscence, sentimentality, wistfulness, yearning.

Cosmic force influencing you
The Water element is aligned with the suit of Cups. Connect to Water today by drinking iced, fresh water from a blue glass, having a relaxing bath, or walking beside a river or lake. Water indicates summertime and the signs of Pisces, Cancer and Scorpio.

Positive action you can take right now
Dig out your old photos, school work, pictures, music, clothes, trinkets, diaries … whatever records of your past you have kept.

THE MINOR ARCANA

SEVEN OF CUPS

Our imagination is a powerful tool. It provides ideas, insights, narratives, solutions, daydreams and fantasies. These passing thoughts can give the blueprints and design of the life you truly wish to lead. Forge a serious alliance with your imagination and take what it shows you seriously.

Daily oracle message
Today is the day that YOU focus on living, recording and researching your daydreams and fantasies. Journey to your inner landscape and record what you find there.

Message of encouragement
Dreaming is free, accessible anytime anywhere, and in all our 'factory settings', and you just need to find the right triggers to allow you to unleash your fantasies. Your daydreams can be powerful embryos of what you most want in this lifetime.

'Dreaming, after all, is a form of planning.'
Gloria Steinem, American journalist and social activist (b. 1934)

Power words
Daydream, fantasy, imagination, inspiration, vision.

Positive action you can take right now
+ Astral travel involves making journeys beyond and apart from the physical body. Begin by visualizing a room that is like an extension of yourself. Make it look and feel however you wish.
+ There is just one rule. There must be a door, through which you enter and leave the room, and another door opposite, through which you pass to your astral journeys.
+ Relax, breathe deeply, close your eyes and mentally enter your astral room through the first doorway.
+ Now decide where you are astral travelling to – this is known as creating your intention. If, for example, you wanted to meet fairies, then say so and visualize it.
+ Open the second door to reveal a fairy mound for you to explore.
+ Once your journey or adventure is complete, return to your astral room through that second door. Turn and face it and imagine a seal of dark earth closing all the seals and hinges of the door so the astral world remains behind it.
+ Take your own time to relax in your astral room and then leave via the first door back to physical reality.

EIGHT OF CUPS

Face your disappointment. Acknowledge where you are experiencing less than what you deserve or expect, where your sacrifices or investments are not being fulfilled or even recognized. Admit it. Suppressing or excusing this stuff is draining and you're not solving anything. When you admit something isn't working, you release that pressure and pain, and you are open to either solutions or closure. Either way, things will improve and change. Don't delay.

Daily oracle message
Today is the day that YOU take responsibility for letting go of something that isn't working. Stop trying, investing, excusing or covering up. It is what it is.

Message of encouragement
Disappointment is a tough emotion, made tougher when you try to resist it and pretend all is well. Don't let failure go to your heart. Admit it, bear the pain, and then move on. Better opportunities will flow towards you now.

'Feast, and your halls are crowded;
Fast, and the world goes by.
Succeed and give, and it helps you live,
But no man can help you die.
There is room in the halls of pleasure
For a large and lordly train,
But one by one we must all file on
Through the narrow aisles of pain.'
'Solitude' by Ella Wheeler Wilcox, American author and poet (1850–1919)

Power words
Accept, admit, concede, release, yield.

Cosmic force influencing you
The Water element is aligned with the suit of Cups. Connect to Water today by drinking iced, fresh water from a blue glass, having a relaxing bath, or walking beside a river or lake. Water indicates summertime and the signs of Pisces, Cancer and Scorpio.

Positive action you can take right now
Write down your hidden disappointment, then read your words out loud. This is powerful in itself. Sigh and expel the feelings. Then burn the piece of paper and bury it. The fire transforms the energy here from physical to ash to earth. Energies will now shift and change. Move on and put the disappointment behind you.

NINE OF CUPS

Grant yourself a wish today. Be your own fairy godmother and welcome treats, playtime, indulgence and joy into your world. Be a beacon for happiness and pleasure, be a magnet for fun and laughter. Make overt moves on your goals and desires, take a chance, throw the dice. Nothing ventured, nothing gained, right?

Daily oracle message
Today is the day that YOU make direct and obvious moves in the direction of the things you want most. Make progress. And be open to lucky breaks and good fortune … anything is possible today.

Message of encouragement
If everything is energy, then you can change your fortunes on the spot simply by changing your mood, outlook and priority for the hour or day ahead. Be bold, feel optimistic, take a chance, put yourself 'out there'. Be like the energy you wish to attract.

'Be the change that you wish to see in the world.'
Mahatma Gandhi, Indian politician and exponent of peaceful resistance (1869–1948)

Power words
Dream, hope, long, pray, wish, yearn.

Cosmic force influencing you
The Water element is aligned with the suit of Cups. Connect to Water today by drinking iced, fresh water from a blue glass, having a relaxing bath, or walking beside a river or lake. Water indicates summertime and the signs of Pisces, Cancer and Scorpio.

Positive action you can take right now
Make a wish. Create a goal, and one that you fully understand. Ask yourself why you want this and find the emotional and spiritual connection to it. Then break it down into smaller milestones.

- List your intentions: 'through my actions, I will …'
- Think about your behaviours and attitude: 'I need to be …'

Your calling in this life is the greatest goal you can work on, and by that I mean working out the intersection of your passion, your expertise or strengths and your usefulness. All three need to be in play. You can't be anything you want to be, BUT you can be everything you are!

TEN OF CUPS

Emotional fulfilment, harmony, peace, love, security and deep joy in your bonds with other people – this is what this card is amplifying in your life, so help it along by investing in your closest and dearest relationships. Make sure the other person knows how you feel, why you appreciate them, what they mean to you, and what plans and dreams you have for your shared future. Jeanne Moreau said, *'Age does not protect you from love, but love to some extent protects you from age.'*

Daily oracle message
Today is the day that YOU focus on those you love and like. Make plans, share compliments, offer help and support, surprise and treat them. Make a grand gesture, even if it's just a handwritten note. (It doesn't have to cost money.)

Message of encouragement
Love is free, is all around us, and belongs to all of us. It never runs out. Even if you have loved and lost, you can love again. Don't turn your back on love.

'This is the miracle that happens every time to those who really love: the more they give, the more they possess.'
Rainer Maria Rilke, Austrian poet (1875–1926)

Power words
Affection, allegiance, alliance, devotion, love, passion.

Cosmic force influencing you
The Water element is aligned with the suit of Cups. Connect to Water today by drinking iced, fresh water from a blue glass, having a relaxing bath, or walking beside a river or lake. Water indicates summertime and the signs of Pisces, Cancer and Scorpio.

Positive action you can take right now
Here are some probing questions to ask a partner, which may reveal important insights or aspects to work on in your relationship.

- What makes you happy?
- What do you think love is?
- Where is your happy place?
- What stresses you out right now?
- Describe your family dynamic.
- How can I love you better?
- How do you most feel loved?

THE MINOR ARCANA

PAGE OF CUPS

Pages can indicate children, so perhaps a child is on your mind, and if so send them love and kindness, and be the kind of presence you wish you had as a child. This card is also a beautiful invitation to be child-like yourself, to indulge in enchantment, creativity and imaginative flights of fancy. Romanticize your world. Sprinkle every humdrum task with a little fairy dust. See the magic all around you and be a part of it.

Daily oracle message
Today is the day that YOU romanticize and enchant your everyday life. Make the morning coffee a ritual, light a candle, wear your best and most costume-like outfit, cast a little happy spell, carry a crystal, read a local legend, look for fairies in nature, visit a haunted spot. Be child-like and magical.

Message of encouragement
Getting creative is a proven, powerful short-cut route out of feeling low, unhappy or lost. Throw yourself into making something or learning how to make something and your mind will get the space it needs to reboot, and life will not (I promise) feel as bleak.

'Art washes away from the soul the dust of everyday life.'
Pablo Picasso, Spanish artist (1881–1973)

Power words
Fantasy imagination, perception, vision.

Cosmic force influencing you
The Water element is aligned with the suit of Cups. Connect to Water today by drinking iced, fresh water from a blue glass, having a relaxing bath, or walking beside a river or lake. Water indicates summertime and the signs of Pisces, Cancer and Scorpio.

Positive action you can take right now
Get creative!

✦ Write a poem or story.
✦ Change your perspective of yourself.
✦ Daydream.
✦ Visit the library and check out new books.
✦ Doodle and draw.
✦ Listen to music while you work.
✦ Go somewhere new and artistic.
✦ Watch comedy.
✦ Meditate.

KNIGHT OF CUPS

Ready to fall (deeper) in love? The Knight of Cups is the tarot's Cupid and arrives in our realm to bring romance, passion and love. Be ready to be literally swept off your feet by a new suitor, impressed by your partner, favoured by a wonderful friend, or maybe just feel a deep sense of appreciation for yourself and who you are.

If you are in a relationship then serve it well. Recognize you are separate entities who both serve a shared bond; your natures combine to each enrich the other.

Daily oracle message
Today is the day that YOU let yourself fall in love. Be romantic and flirtatious, whimsical and imaginative, open-hearted and compassionate, eager to meet and connect with new people.

Message of encouragement
We will enjoy all kinds of relationships through our life, there is no 'normal' or set route to sharing good times and vibes with someone. Seek alignment, seek shared dreams, seek common ground and build your joint empire or realm there.

'Love does not consist of gazing at each other, but in looking together in the same direction.'
Antoine de Saint-Exupéry, French writer (1900–44)

Power words
Alignment, alliance, communication, contract, rapport.

Cosmic force influencing you
The Water element is aligned with the suit of Cups. Connect to Water today by drinking iced, fresh water from a blue glass, having a relaxing bath, or walking beside a river or lake. Water indicates summertime and the signs of Pisces, Cancer and Scorpio.

Positive action you can take right now
Cast a simple love spell to draw your dream lover closer!

✦ Get a (red, ideally) candle and two silver pins. Stick the pins through the middle of the candle, whilst concentrating on your vision of love (whatever it may be).
✦ Repeat this and focus on your desire.
✦ By the time the candle has burned down to the pins, you should have received some kind of message, sign or insight.

THE MINOR ARCANA

QUEEN OF CUPS

You can't pour from an empty jug. We have to prioritize our own self-care. This is not selfish, it's necessary if you're to be healthy, happy and able to care for others too. Self-care is not just wallowing in a bath with a face mask on! It's a combination of challenging yourself to grow, taking ownership of your life's content and direction, and being compassionate to yourself along the way.

Daily oracle message
Today is the day that YOU begin to treat yourself like you would a person you care for deeply and wish to protect.

Message of encouragement
We are often our own very worst enemy. Become your own best friend and you will effortlessly start to share this compassion, mercy, grace and love with others too. Life will blossom.

'I've learned that people will forget what you said, people will forget what you did, but people will never forget how you made them feel.'
Maya Angelou, American memoirist and poet (1928–2014)

Power words
Care, cherish, cultivate, discipline, nurse, nurture, sustain.

Cosmic force influencing you
The Water element is aligned with the suit of Cups. Connect to Water today by drinking iced, fresh water from a blue glass, having a relaxing bath, or walking beside a river or lake. Water indicates summertime and the signs of Pisces, Cancer and Scorpio.

Positive action you can take right now
Take your full date of birth and add all the numbers together and then keep doing that until you reach a number between 1 and 9. That is the number of times you should say one of the below affirmations out loud, in privacy, each day. Do this for at least a week whenever you need to reboot your self-love!

- ✦ 'I matter.'
- ✦ 'I deserve love and kindness.'
- ✦ 'May my inner light shine bright today.'
- ✦ 'I believe in my potential.'

THE MINOR ARCANA

KING OF CUPS

The King of emotional intelligence (the ability to manage your own emotions and understand the emotions of others, with five key elements: self-awareness, self-regulation, motivation, empathy and social skills). The King of Cups blesses you on your own pathway towards supreme emotional intelligence. You are wiser than you ever were. You are experienced, shrewd, worldly, compassionate and kind to others. You are a bright light.

Daily oracle message
Today is the day that YOU put yourself at the service of others because you have so much to offer. It could be something as small as paying a compliment or as large as taking on a coaching role. Seek your place that feels right for the present moment.

Message of encouragement
We so often feel immediately better when we remove the spotlight from ourselves and help to shine it on someone else – uplifting, encouraging, supporting, training, coaching, advising or assisting them to reach their full potential. Feel good by lifting up others.

'It may be that you are not yourself luminous, but that you are a conductor of light. Some people without possessing genius have a remarkable power of stimulating it.'
Sir Arthur Conan Doyle, British writer and physician (1859–1930)

Power words
Boost, embolden, encourage, hearten, help, inspire, motivate, reassure.

Cosmic force influencing you
The Water element is aligned with the suit of Cups. Connect to Water today by drinking iced, fresh water from a blue glass, having a relaxing bath, or walking beside a river or lake. Water indicates summertime and the signs of Pisces, Cancer and Scorpio.

Positive action you can take right now
Meditate on the element of water today. Get closer to water (sit by a pond or river, drive to the coast, go swimming, take a bath, settle down with a glass of water). Watch it move, swirl, ebb, eddy and flow. We are each made of mostly water too. Feel your subtle self, your psyche, move like water. Embrace this emotional flexibility and agility. Feel cleansed and restored by your encounter with this healing, revitalizing element.

KING OF CUPS

ACE OF SWORDS

Aces represent new beginnings and this particular fresh start is activated by expressing a truth you have, up until now, suppressed or bitten your lip about. Truth is often seen as a double-edged sword; it can cut both ways. No single situation is entirely the making of one person or another; we all have roles to play.

Daily oracle message
Today is the day that YOU say it how it is and how you feel. This is the first step to liberation from this negative dynamic or situation. Seek to understand the other person's perspective. Today, all you need to do is to express your truth and listen to theirs. Tomorrow you can work out what next.

Message of encouragement
Learning to speak your mind assertively (not aggressively, nor passively shape-shifting to what others want to hear) is a huge life lesson and skill. Practise your words, rehearse, get feedback, think about their impact. Aim to be clear and honest. Say 'I' not 'you'. Focus on your experience. Leave lots of space and room for their response.

'There are some words that once spoken will split the world in two. There would be the life before you breathed them and then the altered life after they'd been said. They take a long time to find, words like that. They make you hesitate. Choose with care.'
Andrea Levy, British author (1956–2019)

Power words
Accuracy, authenticity, certainty, fact, principle, truth.

Cosmic force influencing you
The Air element is the ruling element for the suit of Swords. Connect to Air today by opening all your windows and airing your home, lighting incense and watching the smoke, or spending as much time outside as possible. Air indicates wintertime and the signs of Gemini, Libra and Aquarius.

Positive action you can take right now
Our throat chakra (where our ugly truths tend to get 'stuck') is represented by the colour blue. You may notice many therapy and healing spaces – and chat-show studios! – are decorated in blue. Use blue today to help channel your truth. Wear a blue scarf, necklace or tie. Use a blue crystal and massage it up and down your neck to unblock and release your emotions stored there.

TWO OF SWORDS

A decision is due. There's no getting around it. Not facing up to it is a decision in itself and will have consequences (probably worse ones because you're leaving it to fate or someone else). Decide what you want, decide what you would sacrifice or compromise to get it, what your priorities are, your timescales, your first step. And, simply, get to it.

Daily oracle message
Today is the day that YOU acknowledge the crossroads in front of you and take control of deciding which path to take. Don't feel paralyzed. This decision is not irreversible; every action ignites a new set of choices. See this as just another step.

Message of encouragement
When you have reached a crossroads in life, taking the new or untravelled path is usually the right thing to do, otherwise why else have you reached a crossroads? Would the path not just have continued?

'I have learned over the years that when one's mind is made up, this diminishes fear.'
Rosa Parks, American activist (1913–2005)

Power words
Choose, decide, discern, judge, resolve.

Cosmic force influencing you
The Air element is the ruling element for the suit of Swords. Connect to Air today by opening all your windows and airing your home, lighting incense and watching the smoke, or spending as much time outside as possible. Air indicates wintertime and the signs of Gemini, Libra and Aquarius.

Positive action you can take right now
Acknowledge the true power of decision making: the ability to change your life at any given moment. Don't leave the scene of this decision without making ONE step in its execution. Look back at previous big decisions in your life and extract life lessons from the process and consequences, get comfortable with the process and judging things quickly. Stay committed to your decision but flexible in how you handle what follows. Unexpected things will unfold – expect that! Be led by your best hopes, not your worst fears.

THE MINOR ARCANA

THREE OF SWORDS

The Three of Swords acknowledges that something has hurt you deeply, probably another person, perhaps by betrayal or cruelty or dishonesty. Whatever their sin, this card gives you permission to fully protect yourself. If you don't like what has been served, then you're free to get up and leave the table. In relationships, you should expect disagreement but not disrespect, distance but not disloyalty.

Daily oracle message
Today is the day that YOU surgically remove from your life whatever it is that has hurt you. Remove it at source. Take ownership of defending your tender heart and your precious realm.

Message of encouragement
Becoming the doer, instead of the done-to, is an empowering moment in adult life. Sometimes it doesn't come till later on in our life, depending on our upbringing, personality and environment. But you WILL know it when it happens. You are reminding people to treat you fairly by drawing new boundaries.

'When you find yourself in a room surrounded by your enemies you should tell yourself "I am not locked in here with you, you are locked in here with me." This is the kind of mindset you should have if you want to succeed in life. Get out of that victim mentality.'
Bruce Lee, Hong Kong-American martial arts actor (1940–73)

Power words
Defend, nurture, protect, shelter, shield.

Cosmic force influencing you
The Air element is the ruling element for the suit of Swords. Connect to Air today by opening all your windows and airing your home, lighting incense and watching the smoke, or spending as much time outside as possible. Air indicates wintertime and the signs of Gemini, Libra and Aquarius.

Positive action you can take right now
Create a psychic shield around yourself today. This is called 'the mirror'. Envision the outer layers of your aura becoming reflective so that anything impinging on it is deflected, like light from a mirror. This shield makes it hard for others to sense and read you. You can experiment with visualizing different types of mirrored surface: metallic, ceramic, white, silver, dark, glossy, matte.

FOUR OF SWORDS

I think of this card as a message to rest. Much has already been completed and overcome. Before taking on anything else, seek deep rest and rejuvenation. You are being advised to enter a temporary, tomb-cool, dark and quiet place, cut off from the living world and let life continue outside. Withdraw from your realm and seek the solitude of your inner tomb. Lie down, rest, replenish.

Daily oracle message
Today is the day that YOU retreat from any and all battles, squalls, challenges and difficulties. Take a time out.

Message of encouragement
Whatever happens in your life, no one can enter or intrude upon your own mind. This is your personal sanctuary, so treat it with reverence and deep protective instincts. Nurture your inner world and you can always find safety and peace.

'Each of us has an inner room where we can visit to be cleansed of fear-based thoughts and feelings. This room, the holy of holies, is a sanctuary of light.'
Marianne Williamson, American author (b. 1952)

Power words
Den, oasis, refuge, retreat, sanctuary, shelter.

Cosmic force influencing you
The Air element is the ruling element for the suit of Swords. Connect to Air today by opening all your windows and airing your home, lighting incense and watching the smoke, or spending as much time outside as possible. Air indicates wintertime and the signs of Gemini, Libra and Aquarius.

Positive action you can take right now
Create a space, altar, placeholder, artwork or notice that promotes the sense of sanctuary in your home. It could be a warm spot by the fire, a window seat, a candle-lit shelf in the bathroom, a cosy, cushioned bed. Create physical sanctuaries at home to remind you of the holiest one of all: your own mind.

THE MINOR ARCANA

FIVE OF SWORDS

Conflict and strife are unavoidable (unless you wish to sacrifice every aspect of yourself to the whim and desire of others, and then the conflict will live inside of you). Handling conflict is an experience we all share. Be brave. You are strong enough to face it and get through a resolution on the other side. Conflict is a teacher and will speak louder and bring more lessons until you hear its message and act accordingly. Your goal is never to add fuel to the fire, but to step back, reflect and consider all sides. Then be a part of reaching resolutions, even if they are simply the bare bones i.e. to part company or agree to disagree.

Daily oracle message
Today is the day that YOU seek to understand a conflict in your realm, get to the root cause, and tackle it at that level.

Message of encouragement
Never act in anger or high emotion. And trust that emotion will always fade, move, shift and pass by. Let it. And then look at the situation again. Buy yourself time to reflect. This is emotional intelligence. This is wisdom.

*'Anger cannot win.
It cannot even think clearly.'*
Dwight D. Eisenhower, American President (1890–1969)

Power words
Conclude, negotiate, propose, resolve, undertake.

Cosmic force influencing you
The Air element is the ruling element for the suit of Swords. Connect to Air today by opening all your windows and airing your home, lighting incense and watching the smoke, or spending as much time outside as possible. Air indicates wintertime and the signs of Gemini, Libra and Aquarius.

Positive action you can take right now
Crystals can help harmonize troubled auras and atmospheres (and give you a point of focus). For instance, jade gently dissolves toxic energy and takes it out of your energy field, replacing it with loving vibes. Jasper cuts old ties and removes dead wood. Rose quartz, packed full of love, rejuvenates and nourishes your emotions and heals any heartache. Block the energy vampires with green aventurine. Heal a damaging childhood with youngite.

SIX OF SWORDS

You are ready to move on. You know it, deep down, and your instincts are correct. The time has come to release something (physically, mentally, materially or emotionally) that has gotten heavy and unwelcome. This process won't feel sad or difficult because it's the perfect moment to do it. Do so with good grace, dignity, with gratitude for the experience or lesson, and relief that this is no longer yours to own.

Daily oracle message
Today is the day that the stars have aligned to help YOU easily, swiftly and cathartically let go of something you no longer want to carry so that you can move on.

Message of encouragement
Healing is a work in progress, a process, for all of us. Indeed, perhaps, something we all live with, all the time, rather than something we complete or get over. You are constantly healing, growing, changing. You are a beautiful work in progress and this marks an important milestone on that journey of growth.

'Healing may not be so much about getting better, as about letting go of everything that isn't you – all of the expectations, all of the beliefs – and becoming who you are.'
Rachel Naomi Remen, American paediatrician (b. 1938)

Power words
Alleviate, heal, improve, release, shed.

Cosmic force influencing you
The Air element is the ruling element for the suit of Swords. Connect to Air today by opening all your windows and airing your home, lighting incense and watching the smoke, or spending as much time outside as possible. Air indicates wintertime and the signs of Gemini, Libra and Aquarius.

Positive action you can take right now
Environment is the unseen influencer that guides behaviour. Default habits love the path of least resistance. Not only does our environment choose that path but it pushes us in that direction. Curate your information diet to be rich and diverse because what you put into your brain now is the raw material you have to work with tomorrow. Surround yourself with people whose default behaviour is your desired behaviour. If you want to exercise more, join a group that exercises daily. Design your environment knowing it will influence your future self.

THE MINOR ARCANA

SEVEN OF SWORDS

Vulnerability is, and has become even more, a currency in our society. We share it in order to build intimacy, understanding, trust. But we should remain prudent, cautious and careful about how vulnerable we let ourselves be and in front of whom. Not everyone has good intentions or is able to treat our vulnerabilities with the care and respect they deserve. Protect your story and yourself; you don't owe your whole self to everyone.

Daily oracle message
Today is the day that YOU close your circle. Identify who you can trust 100 per cent and draw them closest. Identify those you aren't sure about and actively withhold anything that makes you feel vulnerable. Practise guarding your tender heart.

Message of encouragement
You make the choices about who to let in, when and how far. Be your own guardian. Be a protector of your precious self and realm.

'Remember, no one can make you feel inferior without your consent.'
Eleanor Roosevelt, American First Lady (1884–1962)

Power words
Armour, barricade, defence, fortress, guard, shield.

Positive action you can take right now
In tight spots with others, there are a couple of techniques you can use to calm down and create inner fortitude. Pinch the index finger and the thumb of your right hand in the fleshy space between the index finger and the thumb of your left hand. This is an acupressure technique that is great for calming the nervous system.

In Chinese medicine, the space in the centre of the chest, just under the breastbone, is known as 'the sea of tranquillity'. This is the location of the thymus gland, which is part of the lymphatic system. Tapping the centre of the chest is said to reduce stress and anxiety. Join all your fingers and thumb together, as if you were holding a sock puppet and use the fingertips to tap on the chest for about 30 seconds.

THE MINOR ARCANA

EIGHT OF SWORDS

You might have been feeling trapped, thwarted, or backed into a corner. And the (good) news here is that this feeling is coming from within; you are your own worst enemy right now. You are dwelling on unhappy thoughts, self-imposed limitations, and leaning into a victim-type outlook. You have convinced yourself this is not your fault, you're powerless to change, and this is just how it is. My friend, it is not. There is everything you can do to change! Be empowered, see things as they are, and act.

Daily oracle message
Today is the day that YOU recognize and decide to resist the ways in which you imprison and limit your potential. You see the self-limiting beliefs, track their root cause, then dismantle them. Today is about freedom.

Message of encouragement
You can retrain your mind and make it your fuel, your power source, your eternal and ever-positive cheerleader. You can do that and benefit from it right now and forever.

'The mind is everything.
What you think you become.'
Buddha, Siddhartha Gautama, founder of Buddhism (c. 563–518 BCE)

Power words
Believe, discern, envision, imagine, judge, think.

Cosmic force influencing you
The Air element is the ruling element for the suit of Swords. Connect to Air today by opening all your windows and airing your home, lighting incense and watching the smoke, or spending as much time outside as possible. Air indicates wintertime and the signs of Gemini, Libra and Aquarius.

Positive action you can take right now
To achieve something you've never had before, you must do something you've never done before. Do something completely new to you today, something that represents you ignoring your inner judge or critic or self-limiting narrative and proving it wrong. Take action. Seize a challenge. Step into new territory. Escape the cloying comfort zone. Do it now. Prove you can. Break the spell.

NINE OF SWORDS

This card is the most commonly pulled card in any of the readings I do for clients, and I think we are all affected by it every day. It reveals unspoken anxieties and worries, the type of stuff we bottle up and ruminate on secretly, and which grows out of proportion and perspective, weighing us down and making us feel hopeless. We all do this. The trick is to express it all out loud, which proves a psychological exorcism.

Daily oracle message
Today is the day that YOU face and articulate out loud your deepest, dark fears, be it to your oldest friend, a therapist, the mirror or your journal. Get them out of your head and into the cold light of day.

Message of encouragement
Trust that you have overcome before and you will overcome again. There's nothing you can't handle. The first step is sizing up exactly what you're facing. And you do this by sharing it all out loud. I promise most of the dread and worst-case-scenario thinking will immediately evaporate.

'Anxiety does not empty tomorrow of its sorrows, but only empties today of its strength.'
Charles Spurgeon, preacher (1834–92)

Power words
Courage, endurance, grit, spirit, tenacity, valour.

Positive action you can take right now
Centre and ground yourself.

✦ Close your eyes and take three deep breaths.
✦ Visualize a light at the core of your body (that might be your stomach, heart, solar plexus or wherever you feel your core is centred). Visualize a tendril of this light growing down from your core towards the ground, see it penetrate the floor, deep down into the Earth's core.
✦ Draw some of the Earth's core energy up through your tendril, like it was a straw. Let the Earth's energy fill your body.

Use this technique when you feel tired, low, unstable or like you need to ground and balance your energy.

Ten of Swords

One of the bluntest cards in the deck and a clear message that you need to sever ties with someone or something poisonous or draining in your realm. It won't improve. Stop fighting the tide, stop resisting the truth. This situation has gotten too dark, heavy and negative for you to stay put. The time has come to walk away with your head held high.

Daily oracle message
Today is the day that YOU liberate yourself from something you no longer wish to be a part of. Know that you did your best, tried hard and gave them every chance. This simply wasn't meant to be. Now … run!

Message of encouragement
You can do this. You are not scared of letting go because you understand that every ending is the embryo of an exciting new beginning. Summon your courage and make this step.

'Courage is found in unlikely places … Be of good hope!'
J.R.R Tolkien, British author (1892–1973)

Power words
Disconnect, divide, end, rend, resign, separate, sever, split.

Cosmic force influencing you
The Air element is the ruling element for the suit of Swords. Connect to Air today by opening all your windows and airing your home, lighting incense and watching the smoke, or spending as much time outside as possible. Air indicates wintertime and the signs of Gemini, Libra and Aquarius.

Positive action you can take right now
Create a psychic shield today that will help you navigate through this ending without taking any negative energy or ill intention with you. It's called 'the net'. Envision the outer layers of your aura becoming like a web of light with lines that keep out what is undesirable and openings that allow healthy energy to enter. You are asking your aura to filter and discern what can and cannot enter. This is a very versatile shield, useful in many settings, activate it whenever you are unsure of your surrounds or the people around you. Be guarded.

PAGE OF SWORDS

Cultivate mental curiosity and life will always be stimulating. Your mind is your constant companion, why wouldn't you take good care of it and feed it well? Curate a healthy, positive, interesting, varied and exciting mental diet. Ask questions, find the answers. Set up research themes. Learn new topics or skills. Broaden your understanding of the world and all that's in it and you will never be bored or lonely.

Daily oracle message
Today is the day that YOU create a new mental diet for yourself. Decide what you're going to get into and read, learn, try, research, query, or fathom out in the coming week. Start getting curiouser!

Message of encouragement
No one can enter your mindspace without your permission. This is the one place in life that you have total domain over, and you alone are the gatekeeper of what you think.

'The mind that opens to a new idea never returns to its original size.'
Albert Einstein, German theoretical physicist (1879–1955)

Power words
Curious, eager, inquiring, interested, inquisitive, investigative.

Positive action you can take right now
Firstly, a literal physical change in diet can help your grey matter. Make sure you're eating green, leafy vegetables, fatty fish, berries and nuts. Secondly, ensure you let your mind have enough deep rest. Switch off electronic devices in the evening, create a wind-down routine that focuses on unwinding physically, accustoming to the darkness, and letting your fantasies and imagination take over. Thirdly, plan each week's mental stimuli (you can always deviate and add more, but having an initial plan will keep you focused).
Try and go somewhere new, listen to something interesting, try new music, watch a documentary, read a different news source, go to the library, catch a classic movie. Be the curator of your mind.

KNIGHT OF SWORDS

Knights exemplify their suit's characteristics, so this Knight is an ally when you need to be sharp-minded, direct, cerebral, resolute in your opinions and position, and on the front foot when pushing your agenda. You can't get everything you desire with sugar; sometimes you need to add spice! Let this Knight accompany you on tough missions and phases where you know you'll encounter opposition.

Daily oracle message
Today is the day that YOU stand up for yourself, dig your heels in, demand what you deserve, ask for what you desire, put yourself and your needs ahead of others.

Message of encouragement
We all have teeth and claws. We all have what I like to think of (being a Gemini, perhaps) as an inner twin who awakens when we are in danger or our boundaries are being threatened … and takes the wheel! Let the twin take over when you feel 'small'.

'If you don't have a seat at the table, you're probably on the menu.'
Elizabeth Warren, American senator (b. 1949)

Power words
Decisiveness, firmness, fortitude, purpose, resolve, willpower.

Positive action you can take right now
Do a sound cleanse! Sound is purifying, and can penetrate resistant, longstanding and dense energy blocks, that smudging (using smoke) alone can't always cleanse. You can use anything to sound cleanse: a bell, a sound bowl, coins in a bag, rapping on a table top, drums, flicking an empty wine glass … even clapping.

✦ Head to the room you wish to cleanse and open the windows (to release any negative vibes you stir up).
✦ Take your sound cleanser items and shake, rattle and roll them, firstly in the centre of the room, and then in each of the four corners. It's important to listen to the tone of the sounds you create. The duller the noise, the denser and more clogged up that area is, and you may need to shake, rattle and roll several times before the sound becomes higher, clearer and cleaner.

THE MINOR ARCANA

QUEEN OF SWORDS

This Queen represents the place inside you that is uniquely yours where intellect meets intuition, where knowledge is backed by experience, where insight marries up with instinct. Each of us has different 'sweet spots' depending on our mind, background, lifestyle and interests. Recognize yours. Trust your instincts when they match up with good sense. Follow your own internal sat nav, because it's tuned to you alone and knows exactly where you need to go.

Daily oracle message
Today is the day that YOU back yourself. Stop listening to or bowing down to other people's opinions about who you are or what you should be doing. Trust you know best.

Message of encouragement
You are maturing, developing, settling into your life experience and subsequent values and knowledge. This is true personal power. Embrace it, encourage it, use it, actively develop it.

Power words
Assurance, confidence, poise, self-belief, spirit.

Cosmic force influencing you
The Air element is the ruling element for the suit of Swords. Connect to Air today by opening all your windows and airing your home, lighting incense and watching the smoke, or spending as much time outside as possible. Air indicates wintertime and the signs of Gemini, Libra and Aquarius.

Positive action you can take right now
The following crystals are all excellent allies in mental alertness, wisdom building and reflection. Keep them on you through the day and feel their vibration aligning with your own, heightening your mental power.

- **Sunstone:** Promotes positive thinking and self-confidence.
- **Sodalite:** Aids clarity of thought, knowledge retention and creativity, so it's a perfect work ally.
- **Amethyst:** Believed to keep its wearer clear-headed and quick-witted in any kind of skirmish with others.
- **Aquamarine:** Helps to process and release emotional baggage, reduce stress and quell anger.

KING OF SWORDS

The King of Swords exemplifies fairness, objectivity, cerebral power and intellect. I often think of him as like a golden eagle, powerful and respected, flying high above the daily chatter and noise and bustle. He can see for miles, he has perfect vision, he plans his course and flies effortlessly towards his destination. This is how you can feel when you've got your 'mind right', when your intellect is backed by intuition, and you feel ethically and purposefully bound to your course of action.

Daily oracle message
Today is the day that YOU soar like a golden eagle above the heat and noise of everyday life. Up there where the air in thinner and the view is uninterrupted, what can you see? What's important? Where are you heading?

Message of encouragement
When you want to be like the King of Swords, think in decades. This can overcome many pitfalls. If you think about relationships, investments, situations or roles lasting decades, you'll often handle the current moment differently.

'You can't build a long-term future on short-term thinking.'
Billy Cox, American bass guitarist (b. 1941)

Power words
Calculating, devising, engineering, planning.

Cosmic force influencing you
The Air element is the ruling element for the suit of Swords. Connect to Air today by opening all your windows and airing your home, lighting incense and watching the smoke, or spending as much time outside as possible. Air indicates wintertime and the signs of Gemini, Libra and Aquarius.

Positive action you can take right now
Embrace the suit of Swords and its connection to the Air element by introducing incense into your home and surroundings. Burning incense can cleanse your space of negative or stagnant energy, allowing your mind to roam more freely. It can also stimulate different mood states, memories and desires, enabling you to step outside of everyday reality, into a more cerebral state of being. The smoke is also enchanting, relaxing and hypnotic. Burning incense can be the commitment and start of a ritual in thinking and contemplation.

ACE OF WANDS

Aces are new beginnings and today marks one for you, possibly triggered by some good news, an invitation or a conversation that leads somewhere new and exciting! You will feel inspired and energized by what happens. Look out for sparky Fire-sign people. Look out for motivating and optimistic activities or places you can get involved with.

Daily oracle message
Today is the day that YOU accelerate towards the good vibes by activating a fresh start or goal in the areas of either lifestyle, education, travel or creativity. Broaden your horizons.

Message of encouragement
Your ideas will never run out. Don't hold onto them too tightly or think your best days are behind you. Your ideas are a free-flowing service that never stops, a 24/7 concièrge delivery of potential options and possibilities. Share, express, seize, utilize and execute your ideas – every damn day.

'A man may die, nations may rise and fall, but an idea lives on.'
John F. Kennedy, American President (1917–63)

Power words
Concept, idea, notion, potential, thought.

Cosmic force influencing you
Wands resonate to the Fire element. Connect to Fire today by lighting a candle, drawing closer to a fireside, or sitting in the direct rays of the sun and turning your face towards it. Fire indicates springtime and the signs of Aries, Leo and Sagittarius.

Positive action you can take right now
Today is a whole 24 hours you can make your very own. Fill this day with things that bring you joy, are uplifting, inspiring and funny. Take your time to visualize the flow of the coming hours. Embrace the gift of time that you have (that others would sorely wish for, all over the world, right now). There may be ups, downs, adventures and challenges ahead … and you are ready and excited to fulfil your potential today! Go out and live well.

TWO OF WANDS

Focus is everything. Where your focus goes, your energy flows and your lifestyle grows! Often, it's the ability to execute which separates success from failure, not the ability to come up with ideas. You might feel there's too much going on – and you'd be right. You got this card because you need to re-prioritize, figure out your 'big rocks' and put your energy in the right places.

Daily oracle message
Today is the day that YOU streamline your life consciously. Weed out the unimportant or non-urgent. Focus on the important and the urgent. Look ahead and establish key priorities and organize your time, ongoing, around them first and foremost.

Message of encouragement
It's been proven time and again that hard work beats talent (when talent doesn't work hard). That practice is what leads to success. That repetition and dedication are the ingredients of achievement. Know what you want, focus on it. Life can be that simple.

'Focus and simplicity … once you get there, you can move mountains.'
Steve Jobs, American entrepreneur, inventor and founder of Apple (1955–2011)

Power words
Focus, heart, priority, spotlight, target.

Cosmic force influencing you
Wands resonate to the Fire element. Connect to Fire today by lighting a candle, drawing closer to a fireside, or sitting in the direct rays of the sun and turning your face towards it. Fire indicates springtime and the signs of Aries, Leo and Sagittarius.

Positive action you can take right now
Massage your third eye (the middle of your forehead), your temples and crown. Massage can unlock and stimulate your lymph nodes and fluids, like a 'head flush', helping you feel clearer and more alert. The following crystals are all also excellent concentration and focus builders: sodalite, emerald, clear quartz, iolite, tiger's eye, selenite, blue lace agate. Keep them close, use them to massage your head too.

THREE OF WANDS

Life is nothing if not unpredictable. We can go along in our routine, thinking everything will remain as it is … and then BOOM. It all changes. Just like that. This card visits you to help you start practising for those moments, to nudge you towards living life in a more open-hearted, more experimental free-wheeling way. Loosen your need to control things and see what unfolds.

Daily oracle message
Today is the day that YOU step out of your comfort zone and see what the Universe wants to teach you. Be spontaneous, follow your instincts, notice omens and coincidences. Take on a challenge. Step off the beaten track.

Message of encouragement
Everything you do builds valuable experience and, if nothing else, enhances your wisdom and awareness. And, in the pursuit of your goals, you have to embrace the chance of failure, of leaping into the unknown, of NOT being right first time. It's okay. Get comfortable with experimentation.

'Being ready to fail is the only way you get to any kind of solution.'
Peter Barber, British architect (b. 1960)

Power words
Experimental, free-spirited, impromptu, improvized, spontaneous.

Cosmic force influencing you
Wands resonate to the Fire element. Connect to Fire today by lighting a candle, drawing closer to a fireside, or sitting in the direct rays of the sun and turning your face towards it. Fire indicates springtime and the signs of Aries, Leo and Sagittarius.

Positive action you can take right now
One of the simplest things we can do to help our mind embrace the idea that life always goes on and we will awaken to another day is to breathe properly. When you feel flustered, out of control, or stressed, come back to your breathing. Read up on breathwork if this interests you, as there are so many methods and techniques which you can practise for different effects.

Perhaps the simplest is fourfold breathing. Inhale for four beats, hold for four beats, exhale for four beats, pause for four beats, and repeat. Regulate your breath, change your state of mind, regain control, feel confident in the face of whatever life brings.

FOUR OF WANDS

You have worked hard, made progress; you have learnt lessons and tested your appetite for success. Now is a time to build, consolidate, progress, take it to the 'next level'. Celebrate the story so far, really appreciate the good fortune and help you've received, toast your talents and efforts, and look ahead to how you can build on what you've done.

Daily oracle message
Today is the day that YOU pause to acknowledge your successes and celebrate them. At the same time, understand how you can build on them, use them as a foundation for the next chapter, and negotiate a way forwards on your terms.

Message of encouragement
We learn best by doing. Activity is a great teacher. It's often only when we get into something that we understand it and how we can best do it. You are at that point. You have enough experience now to understand how you do what you do best, and what's next.

'You cannot teach a man anything, you can only help him find it within himself.'
Galileo Galilei, Italian polymath (1564–1642)

Power words
Capability, flair, potential, power, skill, talent.

Cosmic force influencing you
Wands resonate to the Fire element. Connect to Fire today by lighting a candle, drawing closer to a fireside, or sitting in the direct rays of the sun and turning your face towards it. Fire indicates springtime and the signs of Aries, Leo and Sagittarius.

Positive action you can take right now
Make a wand! Use it to channel your power and skill by tapping and twirling it over projects, vision boards or technology that you're working with. Swirl it around you to boost your energy levels. Run it over your hands and limbs to stir and awaken your creativity. Simply find a stick that's roughly the same length as your elbow to fingertips, scrape off the bark and sandpaper it to smooth it and round the ends. Adorn it with whatever embellishments or trinkets appeal to you and perhaps represent your talent in some respect.

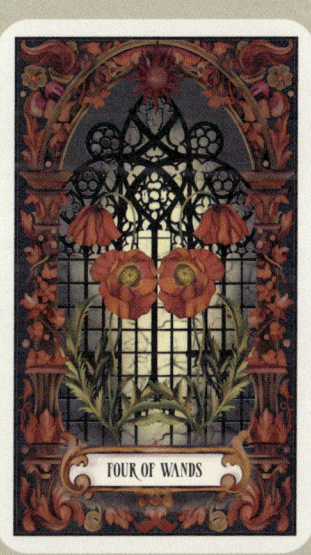

THE MINOR ARCANA

FIVE OF WANDS

Examine where there is tension or conflict in your life. It's likely that this is the first agent of change. Don't focus on the unpleasant symptoms or 'noise', but on the area this conflict is occurring in. What is false, fading, out-dated or not working there? What can you, very simply, move on from to alleviate this turmoil? Deal with it by making a change or instigating a shift or an ending. Something is asking for your attention and adjustment.

Daily oracle message
Today is the day that YOU let something go that has been causing trouble or stress. Letting go, moving on, releasing stuff is free and immediate. If someone has wronged you, let it go. If something isn't working, change it. If something hurts you, release its hold on you.

Message of encouragement
Conflict always has a cause and the shrewdest way to manage it is to get to what the cause is and work on it at that level. In doing so, you will learn a lot about yourself and others. This is valuable life experience.

'Peace is not absence of conflict, it is the ability to handle conflict by peaceful means.'
Ronald Reagan, American President (1911–2004)

Power words
Handle, negotiate, resolve, settle, tackle.

Cosmic force influencing you
Wands resonate to the Fire element. Connect to Fire today by lighting a candle, drawing closer to a fireside, or sitting in the direct rays of the sun and turning your face towards it. Fire indicates springtime and the signs of Aries, Leo and Sagittarius.

Positive action you can take right now
We often carry a great deal of our tension and stress within our physical body (stiff neck, aching back, tense shoulders). Yoga is a great way to release those pressures both physically and mentally. Take a class or follow an online video to make sure you are performing the exercises correctly. Simple poses and movements can unwind your tense muscles and set those emotions free from your body: cat / cow, shoulder rolls, threading the needle, child's pose, bridge, downward dog.

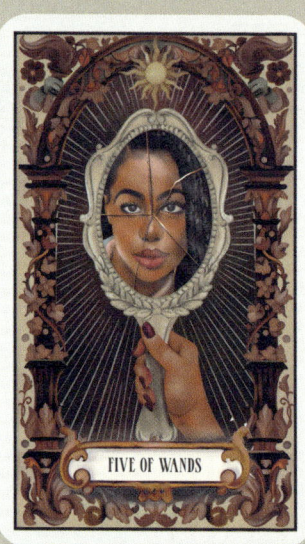

SIX OF WANDS

Be bold, be proud of your achievements, be lucky. You are entering a winning streak, a fortunate phase, a time when you might even feel like you have the Midas touch (everything you touch turns to gold). Use this blessing for good. Help others achieve their dreams and pursue your own. Build on your successes, amplify your talents, do what you love.

Daily oracle message
Today is the day that YOU look back and recognize where, when and how you've achieved success in the past, and figure out how you enhance that in the future.

Message of encouragement
When you do what you love and love what you do, success follows.

'I've come to believe that each of us has a personal calling that's as unique as a fingerprint and that the best way to succeed is to discover what you love and then find a way to offer it to others in the form of service, working hard and also allowing the energy of the Universe to lead you.'
Oprah Winfrey, American talk-show host, producer and writer (b. 1954)

Power words
Accomplish, achieve, advance, prosper, serve, succeed, win.

Cosmic force influencing you
Wands resonate to the Fire element. Connect to Fire today by lighting a candle, drawing closer to a fireside, or sitting in the direct rays of the sun and turning your face towards it. Fire indicates springtime and the signs of Aries, Leo and Sagittarius.

Positive action you can take right now
Celebrate! Make a conscious and overt effort to celebrate your own, and others', successes and achievements today. Look back and list them. Tell people you've noticed what they've overcome or created and that you're proud of them, inspired by them, encouraged by their example. Reach out and compliment people online who inspire you. Send congratulation notes. And reward yourself for your own accomplishments. Let the Universe know that you see the results (and would like more).

THE MINOR ARCANA

SEVEN OF WANDS

Sometimes a challenge is just what we need to shake us out of the status quo, re-focus our attention on what matters (and what doesn't), and bring the best out in us. Competition is artificially created in sports to create excitement for others and targets for competitors. Rivalry can be healthy. Look at where you're experiencing challenge in your life. Do you want or need to win here? If so, get competitive. Create a battle plan. Be a worthy contender.

Daily oracle message
Today is the day that YOU realize you're a force to be reckoned with, a person possessing great strength and experience, and that you deserve to be where you are. Fight for what matters.

Message of encouragement
Challenge is a great teacher. Not only pressure-testing your priorities and goals but also building your resilience and determination to persist even in the face of obstacles or foes. Relish your challenges. Build your character through them.

'Character cannot be developed in ease and quiet. Only through experience of trial and suffering can the soul be strengthened, vision cleared, ambition inspired and success achieved.'
Helen Keller, American author and disability rights activist (1880–1968)

Power words
Battle, challenge, compete, contend, joust, overcome, strive, vie.

Positive action you can take right now
If there isn't an overt challenge visible in your life right now, then set your own (in an area you want to make progress). Choose a target, a timespan to achieve it, how you'll structure your mini targets and milestones in between then and now, determine rules and boundaries, create rewards and prizes, and write it all up somewhere you can refer to it, see it and be guided by it each day. Keep a log of what you've done each day, film and photograph yourself to create a personal record, and stick to your plan! You can do it!

EIGHT OF WANDS

It's who versus what you know that really gets you opportunities in this life – be that via networking, word of mouth, recommendation or whatever. Work on your communication ability, expanse of contacts and depth of understanding, and your efforts will never be wasted. Communication starts with clarity. So many people talk without really getting to a point or saying anything meaningful. Be known for being a person whose voice is worth listening to. This is a reputation you can actively build, and which will serve you well in all aspects of your life.

Daily oracle message
Today is the day that YOU get clear about your goals and desires, understand who can help or unlock them, and work on speaking to those people in the coming fortnight. Use and grow your network.

Message of encouragement
We can all improve our communication skills. It's a personal development project that can last a lifetime and will yield tangible results, so why not invest in yourself in this area?

'Communication is the solvent of all problems and is the foundation for personal development.'
Peter Shepherd, British transformational psychologist (b. 1952)

Power words
Connect, discover, inform, network, understand.

Cosmic force influencing you
Wands resonate to the Fire element. Connect to Fire today by lighting a candle, drawing closer to a fireside, or sitting in the direct rays of the sun and turning your face towards it. Fire indicates springtime and the signs of Aries, Leo and Sagittarius.

Positive action you can take right now
Seek out books, vlogs, influencers, speakers, TED talks, podcasts and experts in communication and read, or listen to, what they advise. Adopt a new habit or trick each week. In general, listen more than you speak, be conscious of your body language, sleep on responding to jarring or emotive messages, write things down and rehearse, pick up the phone wherever possible.

THE MINOR ARCANA

NINE OF WANDS

Whatever it is that is troubling you and you've been dreading tackling ... just know that you already possess all the experience, skill, courage and resources you need to overcome it. The wisdom and resilience is all there waiting for you to tap into it, and you will find this problem is not half as dire as you feared once you start dismantling it and taking action. The Universe has your back, your ancestors have your back, you yourself have your back. Set boundaries, make a plan, take the first step.

Daily oracle message
Today is the day that YOU identify a troubling issue in your life that you've avoided tackling and you make a plan to tackle it! I promise you that you can do this and that this is the right time.

Message of encouragement
You have received this card as a reassurance that you can handle whatever this obstacle is. Things will go better than you think. Action is always preferable to thought. As soon as you start taking steps, the fog will lift and the path will emerge.

'The way to get started is to quit talking and begin doing.'
Walt Disney, American entertainment icon (1901–66)

Power words
Endure, execute, persevere, persist, proceed.

Cosmic force influencing you
Wands resonate to the Fire element. Connect to Fire today by lighting a candle, drawing closer to a fireside, or sitting in the direct rays of the sun and turning your face towards it. Fire indicates springtime and the signs of Aries, Leo and Sagittarius.

Positive action you can take right now
Find out when the next New Moon is (there's one every month). Make that D-Day for getting started on this problem because New Moons are a great cosmic energizer and booster. Between now and then, do your research, pressure-test options, get a second opinion and form a plan of attack. You can do this. You are ready.

THE MINOR ARCANA

TEN OF WANDS

We all have our limit, the tipping point that tilts us into burn out – and we can all sail dangerously close to that line. This card arises in your reading to wave a red flag, to suggest your struggles are threatening to overwhelm you and it's time to step back, compartmentalize and re-focus.

Daily oracle message
Today is the day that YOU will begin to make the right plans for tackling your obstacles or tasks. That begins with deep rest, relaxation, unwinding physically and mentally, prioritizing regaining your strength and vitality. Lighten the load, delegate, eat well, drink plenty, go to bed early. Switch off.

Message of encouragement
Graveyards are full of 'indispensable people'. Nothing is so grave or urgent or important that you can't step back to regain your much-needed energy, perspective and good sense. You will see this all better tomorrow after a day of rest and recuperation.

'Every now and then, go away, have a little relaxation for when you come back to your work, your judgement will be surer.'
Leonardo da Vinci, artist and polymath (1452–1519)

Power words
Calm, comfort, downtime, rejuvenate, silence, slumber.

Cosmic force influencing you
Wands resonate to the Fire element. Connect to Fire today by lighting a candle, drawing closer to a fireside, or sitting in the direct rays of the sun and turning your face towards it. Fire indicates springtime and the signs of Aries, Leo and Sagittarius.

Positive action you can take right now
Plan and execute a soothing and comforting bedtime routine tonight, making it special and super-relaxing. Through the day, use meditation because it is one of the best ways to achieve deep rest without sleep. Focus on a single point, such as your breath, a mantra or a visual image. Grab five minutes whenever you can (they will mount up and have a benefit) to promote calm and a sense of readiness for what's next.

THE MINOR ARCANA

PAGE OF WANDS

We are all, always, a work in progress, until our dying day. You can't complete life, so release feelings of perfectionism or needing to always be right first time and let life teach you what you need to know as you enjoy the passage of time. There's a reset button at every level. You leave school top of the class and enter university a literal freshman. This cycle is reflected in all realms and areas.

Daily oracle message
Today is the day that YOU look back at the last month and extract one or two life lessons: things you have learnt, obstacles you now know how to tackle. Appreciate your growth. These lessons never end.

Message of encouragement
Imagine releasing a pressure valve in your psyche where all your pent-up ideals and must-do thinking are stored. Like an overheating boiler, imagine the pressure gauge falling from red to amber to green. You are under no pressure. Live and see what unfolds!

'Life is trying things to see if they work.'
Ray Bradbury, American author and screen writer (1920–2012)

Power words
Experiment, practise, probe, study, trial.

Positive action you can take right now
Start each day like this.

✦ Sit cross-legged, if you can, and close your eyes.
✦ Run your attention over your body and notice anywhere that feels sore or needs extra attention.
✦ Visualize that area softening, glowing, relaxing.
✦ Next, drink a full glass of water.
✦ Mentally scan your day ahead and acknowledge the tasks ahead of you. Don't think about how you will do them, just acknowledge they are on the list.
✦ Ask yourself 'What am I excited about?', 'What am I nervous about?', 'What am I irritated about?', acknowledge your emotions and their drivers. And say a short, direct affirmation aloud that you feel will give you the power or energy you need to make this day a great one.

THE MINOR ARCANA

KNIGHT OF WANDS

Let the presence of this card immediately change your mood and mindset. Switch onto a high octane, adventurous, anything goes vibration. Do something exciting, take a chance, discover a new passion. This Knight is riding with you to bring an intense energy of impulsivity and challenge to your realm. A wake-up call!

Daily oracle message
Today is the day that YOU see your life as a great adventure. Hardships are trials, here to build character and prove mettle. Challenges are sought. New horizons are the goal. Every decision you make today has the power to change your life.

Message of encouragement
You can't fail, my friend, you really can't. Even a brutal, unexpected setback or collapse eventually leads to hard-won wisdom that will set you up for your next challenge. Never lose faith with yourself or let fear go to your heart. Life is an adventure – live large!

'You cannot swim for new horizons until you have courage to lose sight of the shore.'
William Faulkner, American author (1897–1962)

Power words
Adventure, enterprise, exploit, feat, mission, quest.

Positive action you can take right now
The Knight wants you to light a candle and sit with it tonight. Candle magick is about encouraging and accelerating changes in your life.

- Take a few deep breaths to release tension and visualize your worries or thoughts drifting away from you. Clear your mind.
- Then soften your gaze and stare at the candle's aura (the light right outside of the flame) and visualize it getting bigger and expanding, filling the room.
- Then, imagine it expanding beyond the room into the Universe, beaming out and sending a signal to bring your next adventure to you. Hold this vision in your mind as long as you can.
- When you feel your energy waning, or yourself being distracted, blow out the candle.

QUEEN OF WANDS

Queens visit us when it's time to step up, use our power, take responsibility. In the Queen of Wands' case, she is urging you to design your life to suit yourself and let passion and talent lead you to your natural niches and pathways. Why shape-shift to someone else's vision of you? Be your authentic self. Get creative, seek a fresh challenge, prioritize your interests. Own the life you lead.

Daily oracle message
Today is the day that YOU introduce more of your passion and interests into your daily life – be that by booking a longed-for trip, joining a class, starting a creative project or bringing wellbeing rituals into your daily schedule.

Message of encouragement
When you actively pursue your passions, life gets way more interesting and rewarding, even if there are obstacles or struggles. Passion is the greatest fuel we have to tap in to. Finding and prioritizing your interests, creative sparks, stimulus and purpose is the best way to approach how you live.

'Everyone has a purpose in life and a unique talent to give to others. And when we blend this unique talent with service to others, we experience the ecstasy and exultation of own spirit, which is the ultimate goal of all goals.'
Kallam Anji Reddy, Indian entrepreneur (1941–2013)

Power words
Expertise, flair, forte, knack, know-how, talent.

Cosmic force influencing you
Wands resonate to the Fire element. Connect to Fire today by lighting a candle, drawing closer to a fireside, or sitting in the direct rays of the sun and turning your face towards it. Fire indicates springtime and the signs of Aries, Leo and Sagittarius.

Positive action you can take right now
Use numerology to work out your destiny number. It will tell you what you love doing and how you can bring this passion to life. Write down your birth date in numbers, then add together the digits. For example, 16 June 1984: 1+6+6+1+9+8+4=35. Then reduce to a single digit: 3+5=8. Turn to page 131 to discover what your destiny number means for your life path and purpose. Don't deduce your number if it's 11, 22 or 33 as they are also destiny numbers, and powerful ones.

KING OF WANDS

You are pursuing your life's passion already, or have a plan to get there! You are on the right path. You know what your authentic talent and purpose is; you have perhaps meandered and strayed off course but that's all wisdom and experience now. Others look up to you. Your actions have a wider reach than you could ever know.

Daily oracle message
Today is the day that YOU imagine you are setting an example to a younger you of how to live well, enjoy life, be adventurous, help others achieve their goals and bring light and energy wherever you go. Consciously 'glow'!

Message of encouragement
When you put your wishes at the forefront of your decisions and planning, you can't go wrong. You're letting everyone know what you're about and, even if one pursuit flags, another will emerge because people know what you're about.

'You just go after your wish. As soon as you start to pursue a dream, your life wakes up and everything has meaning.'
Barbara Sher, American writer and life coach (1935–2020)

Power words
Achieved, accomplished, crowned, fulfilled, rewarded.

Cosmic force influencing you
Wands resonate to the Fire element. Connect to Fire today by lighting a candle, drawing closer to a fireside, or sitting in the direct rays of the sun and turning your face towards it. Fire indicates springtime and the signs of Aries, Leo and Sagittarius.

Positive action you can take right now
Start a dream journal.

Many of our deepest desires are played out in our nightly dramas. And the interpretation is often simply 'literal'. Write down your dream in as many 4D details as you can the moment you wake up – who, what, how, why, when, where, what your emotions are, and so on. Look for connections to your waking thoughts or activities. Look for metaphor and simile. Look for links to childhood dreams or fears. Make this a new hobby: a private dream analysis.

TAROT SPREADS

A major part of this deck's appeal is the ability to use it as an oracle deck, simply drawing a card whenever you feel you might need a message, a pick-me-up, a moment of truth or some encouragement.

Using the Cards as Oracle Cards or Single Card Readings

Firstly, wherever you are, try to take a conscious step out of 'ordinary reality'. If you're at home, you can do a breathing or guided meditation exercise, light a candle or incense, perhaps massage your temples or third eye, close your eyes and release any tensions or tightness you feel around your body, particularly your shoulders, neck, jaw and brow. If you're in company, out and about or at work, then maybe you can just close your eyes and breathe deeply, fetch and drink a glass of cold water, or imagine a warm breeze circling your body and sloughing away all the 'sticky' energies of your environment and other people's auras. Some people like to spray a certain fragrance (that's me! I use an energy-clearing spritz or my favourite room-spray 'Haunted House'). Whatever works to help you mark the step from day-to-day thinking to reflection and enlightenment.

Next, shuffle the pack and pick a card. Just one. This is your message for right here, right now.

You may read and resonate with the entire card description or just zoom in on the 'Daily oracle message' and 'Positive action you can take' parts. These two elements make up your oracle reading.

Spend a little time letting that message sink through the layers of your psyche. Gaze at the card as you do so, noticing any aspects that provoke a memory, reaction or association, however abstract or bizarre. Don't try to force meaning over the top of this process, let the meaning come up from underneath, from whatever is stirred by the words you read and the visual you see.

Keep the card with you for the remainder of the day. Before you go to bed, re-read the meaning and notice if anything has changed, now the day is over, about what it meant, provoked or could lead you towards.

Using the Cards for Protection

You can use your tarot deck as a means of protection and that is something we often seek in this cruel, dark world – right?

Find your bodyguard
Firstly, isolate all the Swords cards. This suit is your tarot bodyguard, a fortress you can take sanctuary in and discover how to fight or defend your corner. The Swords suit is the tough guy of the tarot – shrewd, combative, ruthless and self-interested. It represents the Air element and is connected therefore to our auras and what vibration 'gets in' from outside.

+ Firstly, choose your bodyguard. This is the card you will keep close as and when you need protection.
+ The Page is the one if you're seeking protection from or with another source or person or ally.
+ The Knight if you need to fight.
+ The Queen if you need to step up in a new way to display authority or command respect.
+ The King if you are guarding yourself or others to give you a broader protective energy.

Keep your bodyguard card with you for courage. Imagine your court card as a real character that only you can see, walking beside you, watching your back, fending off attacks, lending strength when you need it. You are not alone.

What action do you need to take?
Secondly, use the wider suit to find out what steps you need to take to protect yourself right now.

Isolate the Swords cards 1 to 10, shuffle them and fan them out. Pick one. Then follow the action plan according to the number you have chosen.

1 Have the tough conversation, tell the truth and ask for it back.
2 Make a difficult decision and execute it.
3 Remove or block the source of poison.
4 Retreat, call a truce, withdraw.
5 Tackle this head on. Seek the fastest route to resolution.
6 Leave, quit, end it, move on.
7 Don't trust them. Guard your interests and play your cards close to your chest.
8 Admit you might be part of the problem. Stop projecting your fear.
9 Seek counselling, advice or mentorship. Get these worries out of your head.
10 Sever all ties.

Using the Cards for Encouragement

I believe the most encouraging, empowering, 'you are special and magic' card in the deck is the Magician, so find that card and use it as an ally when you want encouraging energy to surround you. Imagine the Magician is your personal coach, giving you great advice, alerting you to your potential and opportunities that will help to fulfil it, noticing your special and unique gifts and reminding you of them.

+ Try to be the Magician for people you love and I promise you will feel the benefits yourself; the karma will flow. Your ability to encourage yourself will amplify all the quicker when you encourage others.

+ Pop your Magician card in your phone wallet, keep it on your desk, by your mirror or next to your bed.

+ For this spread, place the Magician in the middle and then shuffle and draw four cards and place them from the top left in a clockwise direction to form a square around the Magician.

+ **Card 1:** What is your key strength?
+ **Card 2:** What is your natural talent?
+ **Card 3:** What purpose should you use these gifts for?
+ **Card 4:** How do you get started in manifesting this purpose?

USING THE CARDS FOR RELATIONSHIP ADVICE

Relationships are undoubtedly the centre of most of our worlds. They are the Sun around which our solar system spins. It's important to pay attention to them, nurture them, repair them and enjoy them (perhaps that most importantly, although they take effort, they shouldn't feel like 'work') so they can shine on us and provide energy, warmth and light.

Remember, however, that no single person in your realm can give you everything you need (even your partner) and that is why we need family, friends, colleagues, allies and collaborators of all different kinds. Everyone has limitations. Everyone is different. Take what you enjoy from each person, give plenty in return, and don't place false or impossible expectations on them. If you can achieve that, you should rub along fine.

If not, then this reading might help you get to the bottom of things.

Assessing the dynamics of your relationship

+ **Card 1:** What is the root cause of the current dynamics / situation between you?
+ **Card 2:** What do you need to talk about?
+ **Card 3:** What are the other person's true feelings and intentions towards this relationship?
+ **Card 4:** What should be the immediate action here?
+ **Card 5:** What is the longer-term outlook for this relationship?

Using the Cards for a Time-Specific Reading

Doing regular time-sensitive readings can really help focus and pace your priorities, set a theme or tone for each time frame that helps you get energized and excited and prompt you to look back and reflect and learn from what has just gone. It's an ebb and flow, a building process, a means of living mindfully. This reading can be adapted for any time frame really, but a good rule of thumb is to conduct a reading each week or month. If you're interested in the Moon cycles, you could adapt it for Full and New Moons, perhaps even the start of your sign's season or the New Year.

Remember to write down your cards in your journal so that you can look back and match them up with what actually happened during that phase of your life.

+ **Card 1:** Life lesson or insight from the specified time frame.
+ **Card 2:** What does the Universe want you to know about this specified time frame?
+ **Card 3:** What opportunity should you pursue right now?
+ **Card 4:** How you can help someone in your realm right now?
+ **Card 5:** What was your priority and guiding light through this specified time frame?

Using the Cards for Home Truths and Personal Development

Tarot cards can be a great lens for self-examination, an interactive mirror, a truth-speaking ally who only wants what is best for you. There is no varnish, self-serving agenda or spiteful edge to the messages you can procure from your cards. This is honest and open insight you can lean on and use to work on things you wish to improve or change about your personality, strengths or life experiences.

A good tarot ally is the Ace of Swords, or even the Queen of Wands or the Strength card. Flick through your deck and see if there's a card that reflects – even abstractly – who you wish to become in this life. Pull out that card and keep it close for a day. Try to fathom out why it resonates with you. There's something it is trying to communicate, something you can use as a hook for a phase of personal growth.

The following reading is a good one to do infrequently when you feel you've come to the end of a chapter or that there are conclusions to be drawn from recent events. This reading is reflective and hopefully empowering.

+ **Card 1**: Which card best represents who you are right now?
+ **Card 2:** What conclusion should you draw about a recent turmoil or struggle?
+ **Card 3:** Which card best represents the personal development work you should do next?
+ **Card 4:** Who or what can most help you grow, learn and progress in this next phase?
+ **Card 5:** Which card best represents who you are becoming?

TAROT SPREADS

Numerology

Numerology provides a secret code to your personality, strengths and purpose in life, derived from your date of birth (and also your name). It is similar to astrology in that it's ancient and multi-cultural, as well as being a means of deciphering your character and life path based on when you were born.

Use numerology to work out your destiny number. This is your most important number and it will tell you what you love doing and how you can bring this into your life as a purpose. We often 'grow into' our destiny numbers so you might disagree with what it says about you! There's time yet to mature and change.

Write down your birth date in numbers, then add together the digits.

For example, 16 June 1984: 1+6+6+1+9+8+4=35. Then reduce down to a single digit: 3+5=8.

Don't deduce your number if it's 11, 22 or 33 as they are also destiny numbers, and powerful ones.

+ **Destiny number 1:** Pioneering and independent, born to lead, explore, and chart new territory in whatever field you choose to rule.
+ **Destiny number 2:** Harmony and kindness are your keywords and you are often cast in the role of mediator, healer and counsellor.
+ **Destiny number 3:** Imaginative and creative, a strong communicator, you have influential charisma.
+ **Destiny number 4:** Logical, practical and down to earth, build on the firm foundation of rules but don't be constrained by them.
+ **Destiny number 5:** A restless, freedom-seeking spirited character who lives many lives in one lifetime. Follow your dreams but temper your distractions.
+ **Destiny number 6:** You are a healer and your gentle nature is protective and loving. You seek to resolve problems and tensions.
+ **Destiny number 7:** Inventive and quick-witted and something of a perfectionist, you are a natural researcher and investigator, with a sharp mind.

Continues overleaf

NUMEROLOGY PROVIDES A SECRET CODE TO YOUR PERSONALITY, STRENGTHS AND PURPOSE IN LIFE.

- **Destiny number 8:** Ambitious and aligned to financial success, your pathway begins with determination and accomplishments and leads to contributing to the greater good.
- **Destiny number 9:** Where fantasy meets reality is where you find these spiritually aware people, who sometimes benefit from a reality check. Wise, knowing, intuitive.
- **Destiny number 11:** A spiritual, inspiring, creative individual, often charting a unique path in life and gathering followers and pupils.
- **Destiny number 22:** A natural leader and visionary with the full skill-set to be able to change the world for the better.
- **Destiny number 33:** The rarest life path, the most spiritually evolved and enlightened. A natural healer, teacher and champion of the vulnerable.

Acknowledgements

Thank you to Kate Pollard and Phoebe Bath for providing the means to bring this idea to life. I truly hope this is my masterpiece deck and I am so grateful to be given such support and creative rein on its invention. I hope to repay you with good sales!

A special thank you to my partner in creative crime, Misha Trehan, because this is our second deck and we've shown we can make endless magic. I love your work and your personality. You are a dream to work with and here's to more projects and adventures, my friend.

I am always mindful of the lucky life I get to lead, and I know my allies on the other side send all the help they can. I see you. And I'll see you all again, I know. Till then.

Thank you to Mary Bailey (Miss Bailey). I don't think I'd be doing any of this if it weren't for the positive influence you had on me in childhood; I only wish I could've told you that.

For my family, I am eternally grateful for all of your love, interest, help and kindness. We are a small but mighty unit of different personalities and strengths, banding together through life's challenges. I love you.

For my sister Vicki, especially, who I was with when this deck idea was born, ambling around the magnificent churches of Krakow on one of our happy explorations. You are a unique and magical person.

Luke, my quiet, shrewd, steadfast and wise partner. The King of Capricorns. You have been the difference between how my world was, and how it is now. I love you.

About the Author

Kerry Ward is a tarot reader, deck creator, writer and columnist for *Cosmopolitan* US, UK and *Metro*. Kerry has been reading tarot cards for over 30 years, and has a mission to make tarot reading as easy, accessible and useful for folk all over the world as possible.

Her other titles include *The Good Karma Tarot*, *The Crystal Magic Tarot*, *Taroscopes*, *Power Purpose Practice*, *Card Of The Day Tarot*, and *The Cardless Tarot*. In between creating books and decks, Kerry self publishes journals on Amazon (*The Guided Magic Manifesting Journal*, *The Haunted House Journal*, and *Unleash Your Shadow Self Journal*).

Kerry lives in Nottingham with her partner Luke, and their menagerie of cats – Peaches, Tron and Willow. Shout out to the outdoor cats as well.

Kerry is a Gemini, a bookworm, and a creature of habit, except when she's not.

You can book a personal tarot reading with Kerry in her tarot shop at www.tarotbella.etsy.com, or join her secret tarot club at www.patreon.com/thetarotclub and fill your realm with predictions, forecasts, lessons and guidance from the Major and Minor arcana.

Follow Kerry at @mytarotbella.